BABYSHOCK!

relate

BABYSHOCK!

Your relationship survival guide

Elizabeth Martyn

Vermilion
LONDON

3 5 7 9 10 8 6 4 2

Text © Elizabeth Martyn and Relate 2001

First published in the United Kingdom in 2001 by Vermilion
an imprint of Ebury Press
Random House, 20 Vauxhall Bridge Road, London SW1V 2SA

Random House Australia Pty Limited
20 Alfred Street, Milsons Point, Sydney,
New South Wales 2061, Australia

Random House New Zealand Limited
18 Poland Road, Glenfield,
Auckland 10, New Zealand

Random House South Africa (Pty) Limited
Endulini, 5A Jubilee Road,
Parktown 2193, South Africa

The Random House Group Limited Reg. No. 954009

A CIP catalogue record for this book is available from the British Library

ISBN 0 09 185659 0

Printed and bound in Great Britain by
Bookmarque Ltd, Croydon, Surrey

Papers used by Vermilion are natural, recyclable products made from wood
grown in sustainable forests.

CONTENTS

Part Four: **THRIVING AS A COUPLE**

Part Five: **AS CHILDREN GROW**

ACKNOWLEDGEMENTS

A warm thank you, to all the many people who helped to make this book happen.

To all those at Relate, who gave so generously of their time, knowledge and expertise, especially Linda Brookes, Ruth Cole, Irene Hunt, Denise Knowles, Suzy Powling, Lucy Selleck, Marj Thoburn, Andrew Tyler, Annie Wilson and Annie Wimbush.

To Mel Parr, Linda Connell and John Lewing of PIPPIN, for their invaluable help.

To Mel Tayler for the illustration on page 84, which is based on a diagram showing the Relate theory of triangular inter-action between parents and child, in *Counselling Couples in Relationships*, by Chris Butler and Victoria Joyce (John Wiley & Sons).

To Charlotte Howard, my agent, for her wise advice and support.

To Jacqueline Burns at Vermilion, for all her work in seeing the book through to publication.

Very special thanks are due to all the parents, women and men, whose honesty and insight about the joys and the tribulations of parenthood have greatly enriched this book. Thank you for sharing your experiences and feelings so openly.

And finally, to my husband, Tony and children, Grace and Nicholas – the biggest thanks of all are due to you, for without you I would never have known what a privilege and delight it is, to be a parent.

INTRODUCTION

Children can be the best thing in the world, and the hardest. They change their parents forever, altering their perspectives and priorities. They bring love and joy, laughter and fun, but they also bring frustration and anxiety, hard work and heartache. Children test their parents to the limits.

This book was written because parents deserve a book that acknowledges how tough parenthood can be on a couple's relationship, and which offers help and support in keeping your relationship alive and well in the midst of family life. It doesn't tell you how to change nappies or when to start your baby on solids; but how to look after *yourselves*, not just for your own sakes, but for the sake of everyone in your family.

The most important relationship by far within the family, is the relationship between the parents, because from the quality and strength of that relationship springs the quality and strength of family life. The number of divorces involving couples with children demonstrate that having children is no safeguard against splitting up. Nurturing your own relationship and giving it top priority isn't selfish. It's vital, absolutely vital, for the long-term stability and wellbeing of your family.

In among the demands of daily family life – the packed lunches and sports kits, the endless round of meals, shopping, washing, work – it is very, very easy to lose track of what made it happen in the first place: your relationship as a couple. You might function very well as a working team, servicing the family's needs and keeping everyone else ticking over smoothly. But what about yourselves? Do you still find time for a cuddle, does your heart lift when your partner walks through the door, is there still a spark of romance between you? If these things wither under the onslaught, a few years down the line your family will disperse to lead their own lives, leaving you with nothing.

This is true, whatever the size and shape of your family. Whether you're a young couple planning your first baby, or have children from a previous relationship living with you and want a baby of your own – look after yourselves. If you are adopting a child – look after yourselves. If you have one or more children already and are concerned about how you'll cope with a second or third – look after yourselves.

Maybe your set-up doesn't fit with stereotypes of what makes 'a family', but whatever your particular circumstances it is still of paramount importance to keep your relationship as a couple central. There is, for example, a growing number of lesbian and gay parents, some of whom conceive or adopt children within their relationship, while others have had children in heterosexual relationships before 'coming out', or become the partner of someone who already has children. Although some of the more complex issues facing gay and lesbian couples in having and raising a child are beyond the scope of this book, many of the pressures that fall on heterosexual parents apply to *all* couples who are also parents. Sexuality is irrelevant when you are trying to cope with tiredness and lack of time, juggling work and home life, or tackling any of the numerous other pressures that affect parents' relationships and are discussed in this book.

A baby places a pressure on a couple. This book offers help when the going gets tough. It draws on the wisdom and experience of couples and Relate counsellors to provide you with insights and practical solutions to common problems that you can try for yourself, without a counsellor. No book can be a substitute for the expert help that counselling provides, however. If your problems seem insoluble, or you fear that your relationship is in real danger, then do contact Relate (see page 219) for the support and help that can make all the difference to you and your family.

PART ONE

PLANNING AND PREPARING

Chapter 1

SHALL WE, SHAN'T WE?

I've always thought I'd like children, but it's always been something for the future. My partner and I have been talking and thinking about it together, off and on, for the past two or three years: trying to decide whether or not to start a family. My main worries about it are to do with my freedom in the future and how it will alter my life and my partner's life. I know the sacrifices to be made and worry about how I will cope. Jacqui, quoted in *A Child, Your Choice*

Making the decision to have a child is not like changing jobs, or buying a new car. It's a decision that involves two people intimately and has life-long implications. Making that decision can raise all sorts of doubts and fears which can be hard to acknowledge, and even harder to talk about.

That said, people vary enormously in the way they approach the decision – or even in whether they consciously make the decision at all. Sisters Jayne and Tracey, for example, are both in their twenties. Tracey and her boyfriend Dale have just bought a flat. He works in computers, she is training to be a nursery nurse. They plan to have their first child in three years' time. By then, Tracey will have finished training and had some work experience, and they will be able to afford a house. In the meantime, Tracey is on the pill. That's planning.

Jayne, on the other hand, at 29 has never had a relationship lasting more than six months, although she has always wanted to have children. She works as a legal secretary and rents a flat with friends. Three months ago she met Liam, an unemployed carpenter, fell in love, and is now pregnant, having made 'haphazard' use of the cap. She and Liam have nowhere to live together and no prospect of regular income if Jayne leaves her job. Lately they have been arguing a lot. That's chaos, but it's not uncommon.

Jayne admits that she used contraception erratically because, deep down, 'I wanted to get pregnant. I wanted to try out my body and see if I could actually conceive.' Jayne now finds herself in an unenviable position. Her relationship is unstable and none of her practical problems has a simple solution. 'Now I'm pregnant we seem to have fallen out of love – it's all happened too soon. I want this baby, but I'm afraid I'm going to end up struggling on my own.'

For many women, the idea of having a baby is a deeply emotional one and doesn't respond to rational thinking. Yet the decision has such important consequences, not just for the parents but for the child as well, that it deserves deeper, more conscious reflection.

IS HAVING A BABY RIGHT FOR YOU?

Couples who have been together for a while often find that their family and friends expect them to have children, particularly if they are married. Says a Relate counsellor:

Even though having children may not be right for that couple, people do tend to go along with society's expectations. It's hard to talk about it, if it doesn't feel OK for one or both of them. Having a baby is supposed to be such a happy experience, but there can be a lot of fear of the unknown that needs to be discussed.

Do you both want a baby?

It's very common for one partner to want a child while the other is not so keen. Reasons for not wanting a child can be very deep-seated and include:

- jealousy of a baby
- fear of responsibility
- resentment over the loss of a partner's attention
- desire to keep freedom
- reluctance to make a deep commitment

In this situation, it is very risky to go ahead with a pregnancy, hoping that your partner's views will change, says Relate counsellor Lucy Selleck.

I've so often seen couples where the woman hopes the man will change his mind when the pregnancy becomes a fait accompli. *Sometimes that does happen and the man is delighted when the baby arrives, having said he definitely didn't want one. But people don't necessarily change their minds. It's something to talk about early on in your relationship and, if you are at odds over it, don't assume that things will change. They might, but they might not.*

Think about it

Ask yourselves these questions and reflect on the answers. Babies are people, not miracle-workers. Yes, they do bring many positive benefits into their parents' lives, but they are unlikely to be able to fulfil *all* your needs, nor patch up a shaky relationship.

- Do you want to have a child to please your partner or your parents?

- Are there things missing in your life, which you hope a child could make up for?

- Is having a baby something about which both of you feel positive?

- Do you hope that having a baby will improve your relationship with your partner?

WHAT STAGE ARE YOU AT?

First, think about where you are as individuals. How would your career plans or other aspirations be affected by having a child? Could you cope with the loss of freedom involved in having children? Do one or both of you already have children, and do some or all of them live with you? Having a new baby could place a lot of strain on you.

And where are you as a couple? Are you financially secure, and happy with your housing arrangements? How longstanding is your relationship? Couples need time to be together. Once a child arrives you won't be able to do many of the things that couples without children take for granted: having a weekend lie in, going out on impulse, making love during the day, taking exotic or very active holidays. If you've already had a chance to enjoy a good stretch of time just as a couple, there is less likelihood of you feeling resentful when these shared pleasures have to be set aside for a while.

_____ **Talk about it** _____

- Is having a child something you both feel ready for?

- Have you arrived at the decision together, and has it risen out of a joint commitment to your future as a family?

- Talk about the things you might have to relinquish, and the things you hope to gain.

- Think about goals or plans you have, either individually or as a couple, that haven't been achieved yet. It might be visiting a particular country, achieving at work or in a hobby. How would having a child affect that? Is it something you are willing to postpone for a few years while you bring up your children?

If you are cohabiting

Almost 40 per cent of children are born to parents who are not married. Since almost three-quarters of married couples have lived together first, it seems likely that a lot of unmarried parents will eventually wed. Those who don't, according to One Plus One, an organisation specialising in research into marriage and partnership, run a three to four times higher risk of their relationship breaking down.

How much does your being married matter to your children? One mother who cohabits with her partner and their son says:

What's important is not the public statement of commitment at a wedding, but the private commitment to bring up your children together in a loving way, and to nurture your relationship for their sake as much as for your own.

For some people, the decision to marry is linked to the decision to have children, and they marry with a view to starting a family almost immediately, or when a baby is already on the way. Doing this can put a lot of pressure on a couple, as they have to arrange a wedding when they want to be thinking about their baby, and are left with little time to adjust to being married before they become a family.

We'd always said we'd get married before we had a baby, but we didn't get anything organised until Felix was on the way. I hadn't bargained for feeling sick 24 hours a day, so we had to have a very quiet wedding – just the sight of a champagne bottle made me want to throw up. I wish now that we'd got married before I was pregnant. Claire

A bill going through Parliament at the time of writing will give unmarried fathers full parental rights when they register their children's birth jointly with the mothers. Until that

bill becomes law, however, unmarried fathers don't automatically have parental rights. Even if you are named on
the birth certificate and are supporting the child financially,
you do not have the right to prevent the child being given
up for adoption, having his or her name changed, or being
taken abroad without consent. In order to have these rights,
you must either marry the mother of the child or apply for
Parental Responsibility. This is a free service and you can
apply for a pack containing everything you need by ringing
the Central Registry (see page 216). You will need to do
this until the Adoption and Children Bill becomes law,
scheduled to happen late 2001.

―――――――――― **Think about it** ――――――――――

- What does marriage mean to you?
- Are both of you equally happy with your decision,
  whether you plan to marry or not?
- How deep is your commitment to your relationship as a
  couple, and as a family with children?
- Are your views on marriage the same? If one partner
  wants to marry and the other refuses, it can cause hurt
  and resentment.

INTRODUCING A NEW BABY INTO A STEPFAMILY

More than one family in 14 is a stepfamily and, in the vast
majority of these, the new couple live with children from the
woman's previous relationship. Bringing a new baby into a
stepfamily set-up can be a daunting proposition. A Relate
counsellor explains why:

In many stepfamilies there will already be divided loyalties and tensions between different members, including ex-partners. However much the new couple may want to have a child together, the idea is bound to trigger off an enormous variety of complex feelings in their other children. The children may have fantasised that this new relationship would be short-lived – but having a baby indicates that it will last. Or they may be very jealous of the baby, and fear that all the love will go towards the new child and not towards them. Every child will respond differently.

In the face of all these other people who are involved in their decision, what can a couple do to make things easier? The counsellor suggests that you need to understand everyone else's responses, and not dismiss them as stupid or wrong. Accept that the other children have genuine, deep feelings and do your best to understand them, even if you don't agree with them.

You must also ensure you talk it through, together and with your children. Although you may not win them round to your way of thinking, in the end the decision does rest with you. If you decide to go ahead and have a child, acknowledge your other children's feelings and continue to give them support, love and involvement. This can help them to adjust and, with a bit of luck, eventually accept what has happened.

HOW HEALTHY IS YOUR RELATIONSHIP?

Babies cannot cement a rocky relationship. Psychological research shows that the relationships that fare best under the strains of new parenthood are those that were in pretty good shape beforehand. If a couple communicate well and don't have any serious problems, they stand a good chance of coping well with the arrival of a child. Says one father of two young children:

If you don't want your relationship to change, don't have children. But if you want it to deepen and become more meaningful – go ahead. I discovered a whole new range of feelings and emotions for my partner since we had children. If your relationship is happy and strong, children build an incredible bond. If it isn't, you won't make it.

The hope that a child will hold together an unstable relationship is common. Rumina and Raiaan fell into this trap. Raiaan's job took him away during the week, and he had had an affair early on in their marriage. They tried making a fresh start and Raiaan changed his work routine. Soon Rumina became pregnant, a pregnancy described as 'unplanned', although they had not been using contraception. They came to Relate when the baby was six months old, saying that their relationship was in worse shape than ever before.

The counsellor suggested that one or both of them might have thought that having a baby would help resolve their problems, although they'd never discussed this. Even before the baby was born it was clear that this wouldn't happen. The couple were under a lot of financial strain and, even though they loved their baby, her arrival had done nothing to help their ailing relationship.

In counselling, Rumina and Raiaan worked out ways to handle their money worries and learned to talk more openly rather than making assumptions about how each other were feeling. But it was clear to both of them, and the counsellor, that all this would have been far, far easier if they had tackled their problems *before* starting a family, rather than after.

_____ **Think about it** _____

- Do you have major problems in your relationship – infidelity, violence, addiction to alcohol or drugs, big money worries?

- How easily can you talk about your differences and sort out solutions?

- What is your joint view of parenthood? Are you agreed on who will take the main responsibility for a child, how you will manage financially, what changes will be needed in your lives?

- Is one of you secretly hoping that having a child will give your relationship a level of commitment that doesn't already exist?

DECISION TIME

Some couples, like Tracey and Dale at the start of this chapter, make a definite, thought-through plan of when they hope to have children. Many others drift into the decision, or never consciously make it at all – babies 'just happen'. Gaynor, now a mother of two, says:

I'd never been sure about parenthood – I don't think I ever held a baby before my own, but Tom's enthusiasm was catching. I fell pregnant on honeymoon and, although we both knew the time was right, it was still the scariest thing finding out. I had no idea if I was going to be any good at being a mother. But then if I'd thought about it too much it would probably have been even more scary.

Having a child, like all major decisions in life, carries an element of risk. No one can predict the exact impact of a child on your relationship. If either of you is ambivalent, or if you are looking to a child to prop up your relationship or provide fulfilment that you cannot find elsewhere, beware. Unlike many other decisions, this one is irrevocable. Once you have a child, you have a child for life. Think carefully.

_____ **In brief** _____

- Making a considered decision to have a child is frightening, but it's better than leaving things to chance and hoping for the best.

- Ask yourself why you want a child. Answer honestly.

- Don't rush to start a family. Have some time together first.

- Good, stable relationships fare best under the strains of parenthood. Rocky ones may collapse.

Chapter 2
MAKING BABIES

The day we decided to try for a baby I flung the box of sheaths in the bin – making love without contraception was just lovely. The fact that I might conceive gave it an extra edge of excitement and tenderness that had never been there before. Stella

Once the joint decision to start a family has been made, sex takes on a whole new meaning. Quite apart from not having to bother with contraception, there is a new emotional element which can add intensity.

This feeling won't necessarily be there every time you make love, however, and it can disappear altogether if you don't fall pregnant fairly quickly. Conception is only possible on a few days each month and, according to Issue, the national fertility association, a couple have only a 20 per cent chance of conceiving each month. It can take up to a year for a couple having regular unprotected sex to conceive.

It's best – but hard – to try and stay relaxed, otherwise you risk putting pressure on to your sex life.

After about five months had gone by and I wasn't pregnant, I bought an ovulation predictor kit. The trouble was, that the 'best' time to have sex always seemed to be when we weren't in the mood, or Scott was away. We got very wound up about 'bonking to order' as Scott called it, and after a bit we stopped using the kit, made love when we felt like it and just waited. I got pregnant after 11 months of trying, but it had been a difficult time for both of us. Keri

—————————— **Think about it** ——————————

- Don't be tempted to put your whole life on hold while you are trying to conceive, but if you have major plans, like a house move, organise these before you try to get pregnant. Eat sensibly, give up smoking and take care of your health, but don't become obsessive about it.

MISCARRIAGE

It's a sad truth that miscarriage is a very common experience. As many as 60 per cent of pregnancies are estimated to end in miscarriage, which often happens so early on that the woman didn't know she was pregnant.

Talk to any group of women and you're likely to find that several have had one or more miscarriages. Fortunately, most will also have had successful pregnancies. So although a miscarriage can be very distressing and lead to a deep sense of loss, it need not also bring despair. Even after a series of three miscarriages, there is still a 50 per cent chance of carrying a baby to term.

If you are unfortunate enough to miscarry, give yourself time to recover before trying again. How much time depends on you. Physically, your body may be ready almost immediately, or after one menstrual cycle. Doctors can advise you on that, but they cannot tell you how long it will take you, as an individual, to get over the loss emotionally and feel up to trying again. Miscarriage isn't always taken very seriously by other people, and friends, family and even your partner may expect you to get over it more quickly than you actually do. The experience is different for everyone.

I miscarried at ten weeks. It was a dreadful shock to be told that the baby had died inside me, even though I had been bleeding intermittently and was afraid that something was wrong. I'd become very attached to the idea of that baby. I loved it already. I blamed myself, although the doctor told me that there was no reason to do so – reasons for miscarriage are very often unknown and no one is to blame. My partner was sympathetic but he didn't feel the loss that I felt. And people kept telling me to try again at once. But I wept and wept for that baby and it was six months before I felt like risking another try. I did eventually have a baby the next time, but I was anxious right through the pregnancy in case I lost it. Meena

The loss of a baby through miscarriage can have a lasting effect. It is important to try and talk about how you feel, rather than keeping your sadness under wraps. One counsellor saw a couple six years after their miscarriage.

They had an eight-year-old daughter, but had never got over the loss of the second child they had wanted so badly. They were too afraid to try again in case they lost another one. Worst of all, they had never talked about it. It wasn't until their marriage was in dire straits that they came to Relate. *We talked about grieving and eventually they decided to plant a shrub in their garden, one that flowered in the month the child would have been born. They planted it together, and making that acknowledgement did seem to help them to move on. They left counselling soon afterwards and I heard that they had another baby the following year.*

TERMINATIONS

Many women who have terminated a pregnancy in the past do, later in their lives, go on to have a child. However, thinking about starting a pregnancy when you have terminated one in the past can raise some very uncomfortable feelings. Counsellor Lucy Selleck explains:

A woman may not have thought about her termination for years. Her decision may have been made for perfectly valid reasons, yet she may now start to have feelings about it which she did not have at the time.

Another Relate counsellor says:

Sometimes a woman may be worried that she has been damaged in some way by having a termination, so that she might not be able to conceive now that she wants to. That's when I bring on board the medical people – it can be very helpful for a woman to have a gynaecological check to reassure her that there is no reason to worry. After that we can address any feelings of guilt or shame she might be experiencing over a termination. We talk through the feelings and think about the circumstances that led to her decision. Perhaps she wasn't ready or in a position to become a mother at the time – and if she'd gone ahead, what kind of life would that child have had? By acknowledging her feelings and being open about them, it's often possible to put them to rest.

A woman may not have told her current partner about a past termination, which means that these difficult feelings have to be kept to herself. If this is the case, a counsellor can help her to decide if she wants or needs to tell her partner.

If she does, then she needs to feel clear about her reasons for having the termination so she can be factual when she tells her partner and reassure him that this is a completely different situation, in which the baby is very much wanted by both of them.

INFERTILITY

If time goes by with no conception, you will have to decide whether or not to seek help. IVF is often seen as the cure-all for those who can't conceive, yet only one course of treatment in every five results in a birth. Not only that, but the treatment is costly, invasive and disruptive. Depending on the cause of infertility there are other possible treatments. The first step is to find out what the problem is.

How long should we wait?

Issue suggests that if you have been trying for a baby for more than a year, or if any of the following apply to you, you should ask your GP to arrange for investigations:

- the woman is aged 35 or over
- her periods are irregular or absent
- she has had abdominal or pelvic surgery
- the man has had surgery in the groin, or an injury to the testicles
- either of you has had a sexually transmitted disease
- there is a possible genetic reason

If you do decide to have infertility treatment, it is important to find out about your chances of success before you start. Counsellors often see couples who have had treatment which has not resulted in a baby. Denise Knowles outlines the problems:

There can be a lot of pressure to succeed, both from within the couple and from people outside the relationship, who keep asking how things are going. Sometimes people blame themselves or feel they have let their partner down in some way. Couples can also get hooked on treatment and find themselves unable to call a halt. They can spend a huge amount of

*money, over several years, and end up feeling empty because
the whole relationship has become founded on having children.*

*My advice to couples planning to try infertility treatment
would be to think about what you would do if the treatment
didn't work. Get information and try to go into it with realistic expectations of your chances. And if things don't work
out, get support there and then. Deal with the loss when it
happens, don't leave it until years down the line before you
start trying to come to terms with it.*

ADOPTION

Although it is not right for all couples, for some adoption is
the answer when they discover that they cannot have children. According to the most recent figures, between 4,000
and 6,000 children are adopted every year in the UK. There
are rigorous procedures governing adoption, and your relationship needs to be strong in order to undergo the selection
process.

For Caroline and her husband Bill, there were two years
between making the decision to try to adopt, and receiving
a child.

*We first thought about adoption after I had had two ectopic
pregnancies, and while we were waiting to be accepted into
an IVF programme. I started the ball rolling because I felt we
had nothing to lose. It took a year to find out about adoption
agencies, write to them, receive their replies and be accepted
on an induction course. During this time I'd had three unsuc-
cessful IVF attempts and decided to call a halt.*

*We then waited two or three months for assessment, a
procedure which in itself can take up to nine months. All the
waiting put a lot of strain on us – that, and the invasiveness*

of the assessment, where you are asked lots of intimate questions about your relationship. After we had passed the assessment, we waited yet another ten months before we were offered a child – a three-year-old girl whom we eventually adopted.

_____ **In brief** _____

- Relax, give it time and get on with the rest of your life. Don't pin all your thoughts and hopes on getting pregnant.

- Many, many women miscarry at some time in their life. Take as much time as you need to get over the loss before you try again.

- Infertility treatment can be costly and doesn't always work. Weigh the options carefully, before you go down that road.

- If you are considering adoption, start the ball rolling early on.

Chapter 3
BEING PREGNANT

Well, here I am, December 30th, six weeks pregnant. For the first week or so I felt totally normal, but then sickness, which had been lurking, began to close in. Went off coffee, off wine, off just about everything. Cancelled Christmas, revived, then flagged again. I've got to get back to work on the 4th, but everything feels so altered. I'm in a daze, fit only to lie on the sofa and read and dream . . . And wonder how that little ball of cells is doing, dividing and dividing, safely we trust. Last night we talked names, yet it still seems so unreal – nothing to show for it except total lassitude, a tendency to weep, swollen breasts. Ian is being very sweet and cossets me with soup. What a business! Jacqui

Becoming pregnant is the start of becoming a parent and marks the beginning of a long series of changes. Nothing is the same again from the moment you know you are pregnant.

EVERYTHING IS DIFFERENT

Pregnancy involves not just profound physical changes, but deep-seated emotional responses, both of which can affect a couple's relationship. There can be many hopes, fears and expectations to contend with; some of them conflicting.

I cried when I found out I was pregnant, and it wasn't just tears of joy. I was fearful of the way a baby would change

everything and might even destroy my relationship, which had been the best thing in my life for years. Gaynor

There's no predicting how pregnancy will be for you. Some women find it easy, have few unpleasant physical symptoms, and enjoy the changes taking place in their body. Others put up with a multitude of small discomforts; and a minority may be seriously affected by pregnancy. The women who describe their widely differing experiences of pregnancy here, are all members of the same postnatal support group.

I loved it, just loved it. I felt full of energy, no sickness. Even in the last month I was busy turning the house out from top to bottom.

Although I was reasonably fit, having a baby at 42 was more of a physical strain than it would have been when I was younger. And there was a problem – 'transverse lie' – where the baby lies across the womb, rather than head down. I had to spend ten days in hospital around weeks 37/38 until my daughter moved round into the right position.

My pregnancy was a real cliché – I felt like a contented cow, sailing along with my huge bump. Nothing could faze me, nothing.

Don't talk to me about morning sickness – I was sick morning, noon and night, for five months. I've thrown up in Sainsbury's car park, Victoria Station, at the cinema – you name it. I had to give up work much sooner than I'd planned because commuting made me feel so dreadful.

Pregnancy was OK, but I missed my 'normal' body. I didn't feel like me any more, and that was weird.

In the midst of these changes, it's not unusual to feel vulnerable, or even frightened, especially if you usually feel pretty much in control of your life. Pop star Madonna summed it up:

You hold on to things to get yourself in and out of cars – do things that you perceive as weak and vulnerable. I'm not good at being those things. There's absolutely nothing remotely cool or cutting edge about me right now. And it's very disturbing. Sometimes I burst into tears thinking about it.

The loss of your image of yourself, and its replacement with the new image of a mother-to-be, takes some getting used to. Accepting your burgeoning body is a part of the process, but coming to terms with your new mental state, as you gradually realise how your life is going to alter, takes time. You may be excited one minute, depressed the next.

Meanwhile, your partner will be experiencing changes of his own, and your relationship will be altering as well.

HOW RELATIONSHIPS CHANGE DURING PREGNANCY

At the same time as looking to the future with excitement and anticipation, you'll feel some fear of the unknown. One father, quoted in *From Here to Maternity*, says:

We did have three or four hours of euphoria after getting the test result, but then I remember thinking, 'What the hell are we going to be like as parents? And how are we going to get through the nine months?'

Even if you have always talked through your differences, pregnancy can change things. Mentally, women often turn inwards when they are pregnant, understandably since they are constantly aware of the changes going on in their bodies and the presence of the baby. They may also feel more emotional or tearful, and less able to handle arguments. It's different for men, for whom life can go on much the same.

It would be lovely if pregnancy was a time of total tranquillity, but real life isn't always like that. You or your partner may have worries about work, money, or the impending responsibility of parenthood, which will need to be thought about during this time.

Men's feelings during their partner's pregnancy

Many men are delighted and excited at the prospect of fatherhood. But alongside these positive feelings can come fears and anxieties about how well they will cope with the new demands that will be made on them.

Jordan and Jasmine came to Relate during Jasmine's pregnancy. Previously their relationship had been close and loving, but since the pregnancy Jordan had withdrawn more and more. In counselling it emerged that he resented Jasmine's absorption in the baby. He needed her emotionally, but he no longer felt that she needed him. She in turn felt rejected and angry. What had pushed the marriage into crisis was that he was now having an affair with a colleague.

Looking back at their relationship before the pregnancy, under the counsellor's guidance, all the warning signs were there. Jasmine had acted as mother/lover/friend to Jordan in a way that would be impossible when a child arrived. He needed and wanted that level of emotional involvement, and was unwilling to share her. He admitted that he hadn't really wanted the baby and felt coerced into the pregnancy. This marriage, which had looked so strong, was actually very fragile beneath the surface. It ended in separation, before the baby was born.

Big lifestyle changes of any type – new job, new house, new baby – can trigger stress and a feeling of being unable to cope in a new situation. If a man's partner has become absorbed in her pregnancy he may feel excluded, or unable to get the help he needs from her. These feelings can lead to an affair, or can involve a man simply putting in more hours at work or absenting himself from home for some other reason.

If this happens it can seem at worst like a total betrayal at a time when the woman is at her most vulnerable, and at best like a withdrawal when he is greatly needed. Counselling can help in these situations to unravel feelings and look for a way forward together.

_____ **Talk about it** _____

- Both partners need to resist the temptation to retreat. Keep the lines of communication open and express any doubts and fears you have.

- Reassure your partner that you still love her or him.

- Ask your partner how she or he is feeling – don't always assume that you know.

- If you have specific worries about practical issues like, say, money, try to find solutions together, rather than worrying about them to yourself. Being pregnant can sometimes make mountains out of problems that normally seem manageable. Tackle them together.

_____

Sex during pregnancy

Some lucky women find that pregnancy sets their hormones rampaging, and they feel sexier than ever before. Roberta Israeloff, in her book *Coming to Terms*, describes a holiday with her husband in her fifth month of pregnancy:

Sexuality permeated our little lake-side cabin. The pleasure of no birth control was only part of the story. I was in a nearly continual state of excitement, wanting to make love every day, several times a day and at odd hours, like a kid. Yet as willing and loving a partner as David was that summer, I knew that my bulk interested him only as a change, an oddity.

The physical appearance of a pregnant woman can be a powerful turn-on for some men – and a total turn-off for others. Tricky if you are feeling rampant and he has you down as an untouchable mother-figure for the next few months. For some women, of course, the very thought of being sexually rampant is a rather poor joke and as their size increases their libido dwindles.

There's a lot more about sex in Chapter 15. Whichever way pregnancy affects you both, be prepared for your sex life to change, both now and into the future. As well as feeling like having more sex, or less, you may also be influenced by fears for the baby if you indulge in anything too strenuous, especially if you have miscarried in the past.

Denise Knowles, a Relate sex counsellor, says that couples need to remember that they have a need for intimacy that is not necessarily sexual, and that it's important to keep this side of their relationship going, even if penetrative sex is not on the agenda.

Physical contact keeps you in touch, both now and in the weeks and months following the baby's birth. Get into the habit of touching and caressing each other every day. You can use this time to work on the sensual side of your relationship, so that you are able to have cuddles that don't automatically lead to sex. Fear of the expectation that any physical contact must lead to intercourse is the reason why a lot of people give up on sex. Talk to each other about it, so that either of you can ask for a cuddle – and it just means a cuddle, nothing more unless you want it.

—————————————— **In brief** ——————————————

- Pregnancy is the beginning of a totally new phase of your life. Expect things to change, including relationships.

- Happy and excited one minute, weepy and anxious the next? Don't worry it's perfectly normal.

- Don't back off from your partner even if he doesn't always understand how you're feeling.

- Sex in pregnancy – some women want it more, some a lot less, some not at all.

Chapter 4

PREPARING FOR BIRTH – AND BEYOND

Three-and-a-bit weeks until it's due – the time drags and yet the weeks are flying by. We've still got to re-paper the small room and get some curtains up, buy a pram. I thought these last few weeks of being just us would be a special time, but like everything else it's not at all what I'd expected. There's loads to do, but in the middle of it all I'm rather bored, feel in limbo, miss work, yet don't have the mental wherewithal to do anything constructive. Jacqui

Although the nine months of pregnancy can seem like an eternity, there is a lot to do. There are decisions to be made about work and time off, money questions to consider, help to be sought.

Then there's the practical planning. Where will the baby sleep, what do you need in the way of baby equipment and clothing, do parts of your home need any reorganising or redecorating before the baby arrives?

Some people make no preparations before the baby arrives, often because they don't want to 'tempt fate'. If you're not superstitious, it's a better idea to get as much ready as you can while you've got the chance, rather than having to do it all when you're already very tired and under stress.

There are also decisions to be made about your pregnancy and the birth. As well as deciding whether to go for a hospital or home birth, and what type of maternity care to

choose, you'll be given a birth plan to complete. But before
you reach that stage, one of the very early decisions you
will have to make concerning your baby is whether or not
to have prenatal tests.

PRENATAL TESTS

Most hospitals routinely offer the triple test, which
measures substances in your blood to determine your risk
of having a baby with spina bifida or Down's syndrome.

The triple test can only give you an indication of your
chances of having an affected baby. If you get a result of
one in 250 or more, you will be offered diagnostic tests such
as amniocentesis, which can confirm whether or not the
baby is affected. Unfortunately these tests are invasive and
do carry a low risk of miscarriage.

Although these tests are very useful in identifying affected babies, they do carry their own dilemmas, which each
couple has to resolve in the way that suits them best.
Whether or not to have the tests is something to consider
carefully, together. These three couples had very different
experiences.

*I had the triple test because we wanted reassurance. God
knows what I'd have done if I'd been in a high risk group.
Fortunately I wasn't, but I still had a sneaking worry until
the baby was born that something would be wrong, so it
wasn't quite as reassuring as I'd hoped.*

*We decided to go straight for amnio because, being over 40,
I was already in a high risk group for Down's. We hadn't
made up our minds what to do at that stage, but when the
result came back positive, we knew at once that we would ter-
minate. Not an easy decision, and it is hard being made to*

face up to what your ethics really are. But it felt like the right decision for us, and still does.

My partner and I both felt that no matter what any test showed we would not be able to go through with a termination. We felt that we should accept whatever fate gave us, and make the best of it. So I said no to the triple test – there was no point in having it, because although a low result would be reassuring, a high one would mean that I'd be worried for the rest of the pregnancy. We took the attitude of what will be, will be.

_____ **Talk about it** _____

Many women have a triple test in the hope of discovering that they have a low risk of carrying a baby with spina bifida or Down's syndrome. But as well as bearing in mind that these tests are not definitive and that occasionally women with a low risk result do give birth to affected babies, you also need to think about what you would do if the results put you in a high risk category.

- Would you be willing to have a diagnostic test, with its slight risk of miscarriage, in order to have peace of mind?

- If a diagnostic test showed that your baby was affected, what would you do?

- Would you feel able and willing to cope with a child who had some problems, the severity of which might not be predictable before birth?

- What are your views on termination?

GETTING ORGANISED

Work

Women who are employed and intending to return to work need to organise maternity leave. Currently, you can take 40 weeks off, but only 18 of these are paid, at £60.20 per week. This amount is set to rise in stages and from April 2003 will be £100 per week, when paid maternity leave entitlement will be extended to 26 weeks and will also apply to adoptive parents.

However you decide to play it, give yourself a bit of time off *before* the baby arrives. There are stories of women who are still masterminding boardroom coups from the delivery suite, but the majority are glad to have a chance to take it easy and get sorted out before the action really starts.

The right to two weeks paternity leave, paid at £100 per week, is due to arrive in 2003, and will apply to adoptive fathers too, who currently have no entitlement to leave. Until then, although there is a right to 13 weeks parental leave, this is unpaid, so men have little choice but to return to work within a few days, or at most a couple of weeks. This is the time to find out whether your company offers any paid parental leave – some do. If not, try negotiating, or earmark some holiday entitlement to be taken when the baby is born.

Money

Once you have both sorted out your working arrangements and can predict your post-baby income, you can work out a budget. You might be able to save some money now which would tide you over if you decided to take unpaid leave, bearing in mind that your income will be dropping, at least for a while, as your expenditure goes up.

According to a *Prima* magazine survey, parents spend an average of £4,500 on their baby in year one, and will have stopped using a lot of that kit within the first year. That amount accounts only for a frugal approach, where the mother breastfeeds and clothes come from high street stores, and excludes the cost of childcare, which can dent your bank balance to the tune of £7,000 per annum if you both work fulltime. As always, the key is to talk it over. There is a thriving trade in little-used pushchairs, prams, cots and so on.

If you find it hard to talk about money without fighting, see the chapter on Money, page 129, for help.

Help

Sound out in-laws or other relatives about giving some help in the early days. Discuss this between yourselves before asking. It's great to have a hand with the shopping, cooking and other chores, but you'll also want some time on your own. It might be easier to ask nearby friends or family if they could pop in for an hour or two on some days, rather than inviting relatives who live far away and would have to stay in your home. Set a limit on how long people stay. Don't imagine that fraught relationships will magically improve once you are all clustered around the baby. They might, but you might also feel less able than usual to stand any strains.

Avoid stress

Having a baby is quite stressful enough in its own right without anything being added to the equation. Sounds obvious, yet people regularly organise other swingeing changes to coincide, then wonder why they are finding it hard to cope. And often, of course, life very kindly throws several changes at you simultaneously, and lets you cope as best you can.

Pete and Annie came to Relate because they did nothing but argue. They told the counsellor what had been going on during the last twelve months.

Their baby was six months old. They had moved house in Annie's eighth month of pregnancy because Pete had just gone freelance, as a computer consultant, and so were hardly settled before the baby arrived. The idea had been for Annie to deal with Pete's paperwork in between looking after the baby, but she was finding it impossible. Result: stress.

The counsellor asked Pete and Annie to reflect back on all that had happened in the last year. To them, it felt as if the deterioration in their relationship was just one more problem to contend with when all these other things were going on. They hadn't made the connection. It took someone outside the relationship to point out that they'd had several highly stressful life events crammed into one year. There were huge strains on both of them, and the inevitable result was short tempers.

We looked at each area of their lives separately to see where they could ease up. Pete got himself a part-time job in computing which brought in regular money while he established his business. They farmed out some of the paperwork to someone who could cover it in a couple of days a month, and Annie found a childminder to care for the baby one day a week when she did invoicing and made phone calls. Result: less stress, happier people, fewer rows.

BEING IN THE KNOW

Many people want to gather as much information as possible about pregnancy and birth. There are plenty of books and leaflets around, but a lot of these are aimed at women and are not very father-friendly, and some are patronising or totally unrealistic. Others are stuffed with an encyclopaedic quantity of information, when all you might want to start with are some basic facts.

Antenatal appointments and classes

Antenatal appointments are a great source of practical information for many women, but a survey carried out by the National Childbirth Trust and Fathers Direct discovered that many fathers can't be present even if they want to be, usually because the timing is inconvenient, or their employers won't allow them to be absent. One father in the survey, an agricultural worker, explains:

The appointments were at really awkward times and I couldn't get off work to go. These doctors don't seem to realise that we can't afford to take time off to come and see them. If we want to pay for the baby we have to stay at work.

Antenatal classes, where women are given much information about giving birth, pain control and so on, are usually held during the day, when many men cannot be there. In addition, a third of the fathers in the survey had felt ignored by hospital staff, and said midwives and doctors avoided making eye contact with them.

A lot depends on where you live. In some areas, antenatal sessions are organised when fathers can attend. There may also be the option of private classes, where men are welcomed. With a few exceptions, these focus on the birth and on health details. Little or no attention is given to the emotional impact of a baby on you as a couple.

A worrying time

It's totally normal to have a whole list of things that you are feeling anxious or unsure about. Some of the things expectant mothers have identified as worrying about include the birth – how it will go, how well they'll manage and how well their partner will cope. Men generally worry about their partner's health and wellbeing during pregnancy, their own ability to cope with labour and birth, and how well they'll be able to support their partner. Some of the other things expectant parents worry about include the health of the unborn baby, the impending responsibility of parenthood, how to cope with crying, sleep loss, financial problems and how becoming parents may affect existing problems in their relationship.

No doubt you'll have your own worries to add to these, so what can you do to get them down to manageable proportions?

_____ **Try this** _____

- As always, it is vital to keep the channels of communication open. Talk to your partner – or to a friend or family member if you can't talk to your partner – about how you are feeling.

- Seek information from books, websites, other parents – problems often seem less daunting if you are well-informed. As one father said to Fathers Direct:

  There are heaps of things you need to know about. For doctors and midwives they're just everyday trivial things, but for someone having their first kid it's important to learn about them. That's why books that talk about the common things are good. It doesn't matter if you're not having complications, it sure seems complicated to me.

- Embark on parenthood together with a spirit of adventure – it's a big, exciting event in both your lives. Look forward and prepare for it together, as much as you can.

_____ **In brief** _____

- You don't have to accept ante-natal tests just because they're offered.

- Sit down with a calculator and brace yourself for a shock. Babies cost money.

- Take control, and get yourself informed about what to expect during pregnancy and birth.

- Simplify the rest of your life as much as possible.

PART TWO

FROM PARTNERS
TO PARENTS

Chapter 5

BIRTH: A NEW BEGINNING

Eventually they told me to push and I pushed with all my might and at last, 'There's the head, there's the head,' said Graham, all excited. They propped me up and I caught a glimpse of a wet, hair-covered head emerging. 'One more push.' I pushed and wept. Our baby was being born. And suddenly the baby was there and they put her on a cloth on my tummy. A beautiful girl . . . Later, down in the ward, we were all together and I suddenly felt totally overwhelmed. I had a daughter, a beautiful, beautiful daughter. And Graham was also caught up in it – his delight in the baby, and his pride in me. He said I'd done very well in labour and I felt I had, too. It was lovely having him there. It gave me strength. Sian, mother of Daisy

Giving birth is one of life's most powerful experiences. It is the threshold that must be crossed before you can be admitted to the world of parenthood. It is also an unpredictable event. No one can say in advance what your labour will be like. But you can think ahead about how you as a couple would like to share the experience of your child's birth.

FATHERS AT THE BIRTH

Around 90 per cent of fathers are present at the births of their children. For many – but not for all – the experience is a good, or at least tolerable, one, and all in all they are glad to have been there. Novelist Sean French, writing in a newspaper feature, describes his feelings:

It felt intensely important for both of us that I was there. For nine months the child had been my wife's. She had been the one throwing up and wobbling around. Now, from the moment the baby was born, it was going to be ours. This was one of the main events of our life together and it would feel strange not to experience it together.

Because such a high proportion of fathers do attend the birth, however, there is a pressure on all men to be there, even if the last place on earth they'd really want to be is in a delivery suite. Gavin, when his wife was eight months pregnant, said:

My first reaction was 'Arghh! I don't want to be there. I'd probably faint, I'm pretty squeamish.' Fortunately my wife agrees, she wants her best friend there instead – she says giving birth is traditionally a women's thing and she'd rather I kept out of it.

If the man is reluctant, the woman may have mixed feelings about having him there. Cheryl says:

My husband didn't really want to come, but there was no one else available. I wanted to have someone with me to complain to medical staff if anything went wrong. In the event, I had an emergency Caesarean, with full anaesthetic, and he was told to wait outside. I think he was quite relieved, and I was too, in a way.

All is revealed

Some men feel uncomfortable with the woman's physical exposure during birth. Psychologist Anne Woollett explains:

During birth, a woman's genitals are displayed to the world. In a relationship, they are exposed only to her partner. It is hard from some men to share that with a male doctor and it can affect a couple's sex life.

Sexual response is a highly individual thing. While some men may be sexually turned off for a while after watching their partner give birth, or be afraid of hurting her, others find that seeing their partner in the throes of such a powerful physical experience actually enhances their sexual attraction to her. There's more on how a couple's sex life alters after the birth of a child in Chapter 15, page 153.

I'm in charge

Seeing a woman give birth can be frightening. Some men respond by trying to take command in order to regain a sense of control. This is pretty unhelpful for the woman, who can only do what her body tells her. Other men question staff relentlessly. Childbirth guru Michel Odent believes that some men, in their anxiety for the woman, try to talk rationally to her, but by doing so they distract her and pass on their own fear. Women, he says, may be better off giving birth accompanied by another woman who has had a child.

Despite all this adverse comment, for many couples sharing the birth creates a strong bond, both between the couple and between them and the baby. For women like Sian, quoted at the start of this chapter, the presence of their partner during labour makes them feel greatly loved and supported.

For many men, seeing their child born is one of the highest points in their life. Graham, Sian's husband, describes his experience:

It was unbelievable. I was running round getting water for Sian, and trying to help out with the midwife. She asked me to do a couple of things, and I was really participating. And I was the first one to see she was a girl, even before the doctor. You just get used to all the machines and instruments and stuff. I felt really emotional. It was like seeing a good film: you want to see it again.

_____ **Talk about it** _____

- Never mind what anyone else thinks or expects you to do. Each couple has to decide for themselves how to approach the birth and do what intuitively feels right.

- If a man feels ambivalent about being at the birth, it can help to talk about his fears, perhaps to another man who has already witnessed a birth.

- Ultimately, the woman ought to have the final say on who is present at the birth with her.

AFTER THE BIRTH

Labour is so all-engulfing that it can take some time afterwards to realise fully what has just happened. Anne Oakley, in her book *From Here to Maternity*, interviewed new mothers about their feelings immediately after giving birth:

Birth is a trauma in every sense of the word. Physical lacerations ensue, but the mind and the emotions are wounded as well by the immensity of the physical sensations felt and by their meaning: another human being. The word 'shock' was used over and over again by the women interviewed, in comments such as:

'It is a state of shock. I was unaware – I mean I'd like to have another one, just to be aware of what's going on.'

'He was so big . . . nine pounds six . . . I was absolutely shocked out of my mind.'

'I felt depressed in hospital. It was partly shock really, and being away from home.'

The post-birth hours and days can go by in a fog of mixed feelings. It is common to have swings of emotion. Some women are turfed out of hospital before they feel really ready, while others stay in for longer than they would choose, like Sian:

I spent five days in hospital, while Daisy recovered from jaundice. To begin with it was OK – the midwives helped with feeding (agony to start with), nappy changing, etc. But it was so hot, and so hard to sleep in a six-bed ward with all the other babies crying. I ended up so tired. On Friday morning I begged to be allowed to go home. Finally at 7pm they said I could go (by then I'd rung Graham in tears and said 'I'm discharging myself') and by 7.30 we were out.

However things pan out, men can do a lot to make time in hospital, or an early arrival back home, easier for their partners.

_____ **Try this** _____

- Ask people to check with you before visiting hospital and to keep their visits brief.

- Line up help from relatives or friends to tide you over in the first few days or weeks.

- If you have a few days alone before your partner and the baby come home, catch up on your own sleep so that at least one of you feels rested.

- Take the opportunity to stock up on food and get the house as clean and tidy as you can.

- Once you know when your partner and the baby are coming home, set aside some time when you can be on your own together as a new family, getting to know your new baby.

WHEN SOMETHING GOES WRONG

Ask expectant parents about their baby before it is born and the majority will say that they don't mind what sex it is, or what it looks like, 'as long as it's all right'. It's natural to want your child to be fit and healthy. Unfortunately, though, sometimes a baby is born less than perfect.

The range of problems is wide. Some are easily rectified, while others have long-term implications. In either case, the shock of giving birth to a child who is damaged or ailing in some way, is profound.

Andy Merriman's daughter Sarah was born with Down's syndrome. He wrote a book about the experience, *A Minor Adjustment*, in which he quotes his wife Allie's thoughts on the day of Sarah's birth.

Later Andy returned with our son Daniel. 'What have I done to you?' I whispered to myself as he came running in to see his new sister. I had planned not to be holding my second baby when Daniel visited, as all the books said this could help reduce the levels of jealousy in the older sibling. That was one problem I didn't have. I wasn't holding her because I didn't feel like holding her. For Daniel's sake I tried to look happy, but inside I was full of dread.

Grief and anger are natural, strong responses in cases like these. Even if these feelings alter in time, in the early days they can be hard to handle. Counsellor Denise Knowles has helped couples in this situation.

The feelings of loss and failure are huge. Couples look for support and help, but often people scatter and are very embarrassed because they just can't handle it. If no one will talk about what has happened, very soon you become full of unresolved anger at the people who are not there for you.

It's common, says Denise, for couples not even to be able to help each other at this time.

They retreat into their own corners and don't share their grief. I try to help them see that they are not doing each other any favours by appearing to be so strong and coping. They need to acknowledge their weakness together. Another problem is that partners make assumptions about each other which widen the gap even further. A man will say to me, 'I'm not going to her because she's coping all right.' But that may not be the truth.

Over time, says Denise, couples can come to take a more positive view.

People need to realise that they owe it to themselves to come to terms with what has happened and get over it. They certainly owe it to their child. They can develop new skills and talents looking after that child and grasp the opportunity to learn and help their family and friends to be less opinionated about handicap.

When a baby dies

Although childbirth is far safer than it was even fifty years ago, and medical advances mean that many babies survive who would not have done in the past, it is still a sad fact that around nine babies in every thousand are born dead or die within the first four weeks of life.

The parents of these babies have a hard task to face. All their hopes and expectations have been lost and finding a way forward can seem impossible. Wrote one bereaved mother:

So many agonising feelings. The real longing for her just to be here, to be able to hold and cuddle her.

Everyone has different needs. Some people are helped by talking to someone else whose baby has died, others by gathering information on the causes of death. Some take support from a help-group such as SANDS (see page 219). Yet others respond by withdrawing from the world, until they feel ready to face other people again. It can be hard for couples to help each other in this situation. Denise Knowles explains:

When a couple experience the loss of a child it can close down communication. The loss has had an impact at a very deep level, and they lose the ability to talk about it. They may be desperate for another child, but full of fear that the same thing will happen again. It can help to recognise the loss fully and go with those feelings. Allow yourselves to grieve, make recognition of the lost child in some way, perhaps by making some lasting memorial. In time, you may be able to move away from the loss and think about planning for another child if that is what you want to do.

In brief

- Even reluctant dads get a lot out of being present at the birth.

- Ease up in the very early days – limit visitors, organise help, coast along together in the chaos of life with a new baby.

- It's a terrible shock to give birth to a child who is less than perfect, or to lose a child at birth. Couples can't always comfort each other at first if this happens.

Chapter 6

HOME AT LAST

The trick is to snatch moments when you can, to learn to do things with one hand, to learn not to fret when all you can do is sit with him on your lap or at the breast and nothing else gets done for hours and hours. Any semblance of normality has gone out of the window – we live on frozen meals, the table is thick with unopened post, the washing basket is overflowing, the bed unmade. Now I know why new mothers spend all day in their dressing gowns – it's because babies take up ALL your time. Haylie, mother of two-week-old Calum

No one can prepare you adequately for the reality of having a baby. Routines disintegrate, emotions waver, your body may be tender and painful, the house is full of baby equipment and in the midst of it all you are trying to cope with this fragile and demanding little creature on whom everything is suddenly focused. Nothing is the same as it was before the birth. To say the learning curve is steep is misleading – it is perpendicular. It is the most intense of experiences, the most demanding, the most all engulfing. Wonderful, but shattering in every sense of the word.

Part of the shock is an emotional rawness that can leave you feeling vulnerable and overwhelmed. Susan Johnson, in her book *A Better Woman*, writes:

A new baby craves nothing less than the whole of its mother, a mother's arms, a mother's body, a mother's milk, a

*mother's sleep. A new baby takes the sleep from your eyes,
the breath from your lungs, a new baby requires that you
lay your body down as the bridge on which he will learn to
stand.*

No one else asks as much as a newborn. No matter how
much you wanted your baby, the enormity of the demand
still comes as a shock.

There's an earthiness about having a new baby, too,
which is far removed from most people's sanitised ex-
istences. Haylie remembers a scene from the second week of
her son's life.

*We were sitting at the breakfast table, and I was expressing
milk with a hand-held breast pump. The milk jetted out –
squirt, squirt – and Mike said, 'Now you know how a cow
feels,' which didn't strike me as funny. I had to perch on the
edge of the chair because my rear end was a mass of bruises
from the forceps delivery, and I was wearing a milk-stained
nightie; under it a vast pair of pants to fit round my bulging
tummy, holding a sanitary towel because I was still bleeding
from the birth and couldn't use my normal tampons. I felt
highly glamorous, as you can imagine. Mike was wearing his
suit, because he was just about to go off to work. He was
holding Calum while I expressed when, without warning,
Calum's face turned puce. There was a loud squelching
noise, and a stream of mustard-coloured poo shot out of his
nappy all down Mike's trousers. We laughed, but I could just
as easily have cried. What had happened to us?*

Having a child is a huge, real experience that alters everything, and that in itself is exciting. Bringing your baby
home puts you face to face with the reality of total change.
That's exciting too, but it can also feel terrifying.

LIFE WITH A NEWBORN

Family life kicks in the minute you are first at home, alone, with your baby. From this moment on you are a family, though it can take a while to get used to that idea. Here are some thoughts from four parents, with four very different babies, about how they felt in those early weeks.

I almost tried to pretend nothing had happened. I came home from hospital within a few hours after 24 hours-plus of exhausting labour and I was up and dressed doing a superwoman act for everyone to see. I pretended I was a natural at breastfeeding (I ignored advice and never did master it) and seemed intent to prove to everyone how easy it was to have a baby. Gaynor

To start with, Anvesh was very contented, and always settled down to sleep early in the evening. In that first week I can remember sitting with my husband having a beer and watching East-Enders, *saying, 'I don't know why people say that babies change your life.' Ten days later he developed colic, and that was it – no more peaceful evenings. I haven't seen* EastEnders *since.* Shipra

One afternoon, I got so tired I completely lost my rag because Julie didn't leave the room with Savannah when she started crying when I'd fallen asleep. I flung a potato at her, yelling 'You're so bloody inconsiderate'. That's not like me at all. Andy

Having this baby, it's like being in love. There's a feeling of excitement, just like the start of an affair. A physical enrapturement, loving her perfect little body, loving to hold and cuddle her. The sound of her voice, even when she's crying – I just love it. Karen

What a range of emotions. What a range of experiences. What a shock to a couple's relationship.

Imagine if anyone other than your baby moved in with you, and one of you fell in love. How would the other partner feel? Suppose this stranger kept you awake half the night, behaved unpredictably, cried for hours on end and refused to be comforted? How would you cope? What would that do to your relationship?

As parents, most people do discover astonishing reserves of patience and resilience they never knew they had. They also experience moments of intense emotion – anger, guilt, frustration – that can leave them shaken or afraid.

Many relationships go through an emotional earthquake when a baby arrives, as feelings skid backwards and forwards along a scale that ranges from bliss to rage.

The most obvious stress that a new baby puts on the household is the total demolition of normal routines. Couple this with the challenge of coping with crying, against a background of lost sleep, and you start to see why those first few weeks can be pretty tough.

Try this

- If you don't feel a bond with your baby straight away, give yourself time. It can happen suddenly or gradually, but it will happen.

- Many women feel angry – with the baby, when he refuses to cooperate; with their partner for not helping enough; with themselves, for not coping, or for feeling angry at all. All very normal and understandable, and often very alarming. If your feelings threaten to escalate out of control, give yourself a change of scene. Take the baby out in the pram or for a drive, or call a friend and get some company.

- If you're afraid that anger could make you violent, get away quickly until you are calmer – even just going into another room or outside for a few minutes can soothe your nerves.

- Don't keep it all to yourself. Talk to your partner, and to other parents – you'll find that many of them are experiencing the same mixture of conflicting feelings.

Loss of routine

It's hard – no, it's impossible – to imagine how thoroughly babies upend normal life. Breastfeeding particularly can occupy hours and hours. For a while all activity revolves around the baby's sleeping and feeding patterns, and everything else has to fit in, or be forgotten.

And that's the rub. We are so used to cramming so much into every hour, that to be prevented from doing so can feel wildly frustrating. One mother recalled weeping while she fed her baby son, 'because I couldn't think when I would catch up with the ironing.' Sounds crazy, maybe, but if instead of ironing, you read – 'when I would catch up with my life again' – it makes perfect sense.

_____ **Try this** _____

- Take practical steps to ease your daily life. Fill the freezer with prepared meals. Cut down on non-essential tasks and persuade, or pay, others to do the essentials for you.

- Accept all offers of help and ask people to do the specific jobs that would be the most useful.

- Know that this is not forever. The wonder of the tiny-baby phase is that it is shortlived. By six months your baby will be sitting up, starting to play, eating at reasonable intervals, sleeping for longer periods. The bundle in the shawl will have been and gone. While it lasts, be forgiving of yourself. Enjoy the baby and let other routines hang for the time being.

- Accept that you cannot be super-efficient at the moment.

- Try to get people around you – family, friends, neighbours – to understand that you must meet the baby's needs first for the time being.

Crying babies

Life with a baby that cries a lot is exhausting; a huge
challenge at a time when you're least able to respond. The
sound of a baby crying is *meant* to go right through you.
Nature planned it that way, although this is scant comfort
when your baby's yells make you feel as if you are being
attacked with a chainsaw.

Tim found it easier to live with Nathan's evening crying
bouts once he had realised why babies cry.

*I found it easier to deal with crying after we had talked about
it at a postnatal support group. The leader explained that
babies have very few ways to communicate, and that crying is
one of the most important. Think what it must be like if
you're frightened, uncomfortable, or in pain, and there's no
way to tell the people who look after you what the problem is.
Next time Nathan cried, I heard it in a different way. He
needed help, and I was there to help him. Understanding that
made a huge difference – crying and comforting began to
feel like a dialogue between us.*

Don't worry if you can't make that leap to dialogue all at
once, or if some days it all seems easier than others. Sian,
mother of 8-week-old Daisy writes:

*One night D howled until 2am. In the end I thrust her down,
yelling 'Go to sleep!', then burst into tears. Graham took over
and calmed us both. When that happens I feel like a child
myself and want him to say, 'Won't that nasty baby stop
crying? Poor Sian,' and comfort me, not her. Fortunately he
doesn't. He attends to Daisy first, then says 'It's only a
baby crying – don't take it as a personal insult.' That
night was the end of my honeymoon with Daisy though, and
the start of a realisation that I must be more mature myself,
for her.*

- Hold on to the belief that this phase will pass. Your baby will not still be crying like this in six months' time.
- Work with your partner to support each other through it. Take turns with the baby. When it's not your turn, don't hover – get away from the noise. Go out, if need be.
- Get help. Leave the baby with a relative or friend whom you trust and have a complete break for an hour.

Sleep, glorious sleep

What can you do to combat the effects of broken nights? The brunt of these generally falls on women, according to research done for *Mother and Baby* magazine, which found that only 17 per cent of new fathers regularly got up to comfort a crying baby, and about the same number never stir from their slumbers at all. If a woman is breastfeeding, of course, there's little her partner can do to help, even if he does get up. If she isn't, then it seems only fair that her partner take over for at least some of the time, although many women find that they wake up the instant the baby murmurs and can't get back to sleep again until they're sure the baby is settled, so they might as well get up.

Whether getting up in the night is something you can share or not, one or both of you is going to end up feeling pretty exhausted. Joanna Briscoe, writing in a newspaper article, recalled the sensation of extreme exhaustion:

Black spots in front of the eyes, faint hallucinations, the fear of vomiting from tiredness, the whole body a vibrating, empty chamber of panic. Your head is composed of shifting sand. Your mind is grainy, buzzing, separated from the world by a layer of scum. It functions only for the obsessive calculation of available sleep.

No wonder sleep deprivation has been used as a form of torture. You simply cannot expect to function properly while you are suffering from it, and consequently must be as easy on yourself as you possibly can until things get better. Haylie says:

Calum woke numerous times every night, and didn't sleep through until he was nine months. Exhaustion affected everything I did. At times I was so tired I thought I might die from it.

_____ **Try this** _____

Not all babies wake as often as Calum, and some sleep through the night much sooner. All babies rob their parents of some sleep though, so until nights improve – and they *do* improve:

- Be kind to yourself and each other, knowing that lack of sleep causes lowered tolerance and frayed tempers.

- Try every ploy you can to get your baby to sleep better – read baby books, ask friends for suggestions – one of them might do the trick for your child. At the same time, realise that there is no magic technique that works for all babies, and you may just have to wait it out.

- Line up grandparents, friends, anyone who could push the pram round the park for an hour or two while you rest.

- Forget about keeping the house immaculate, and put ambitious plans for, say, travel or decorating on hold for a while.

- Rest whenever you can. Practise saying 'no' to other people's demands, and put your own need for sleep high on the agenda.

- Sleeping separately can help to keep at least one of you

from falling apart, but don't do it for too long. Chantal, mother of five-week-old Florence, says:

Gavin is still sleeping downstairs – very necessary, as nights are so broken. One of us needs a few undisturbed hours. But I miss him.

Sharing a bed is an important part of being a couple. Bed is where intimate conversations take place. It can be the place for reconciliation if you've fallen out during the day. And when it comes to getting back to sex, there's little hope if you're not even sharing a bed.

In brief

- Some mothers are on a high, others feel totally numb. You'll spend the first weeks on an emotional yo-yo.

- Slow down, slow down. Let the baby dictate the pace – it's the only way to stay sane.

- Crying is like toothache – wonderful when it stops. And stop it does, as babies mature, so hang on, it's not for ever.

- Lack of sleep makes the simplest tasks seem impossible. Accept it, and go easy on yourself.

Chapter 7

MOTHERHOOD: A MASS OF CONTRADICTIONS

Five days after Connor was born, I remember watching care-free young women students cycling up the road, while I had a crying baby, breasts like boulders, stitches and piles. I had a real pang of envy, feeling there was no turning back now I had responsibility for this child, and wondering if I'd ever sit on a bicycle again! Beth

There are many, many changes to take on board when you become a mother. Many of these creep up gradually. For the first week or two there is often plenty of help around. Later, when partners have gone back to work, in-laws have decamped and you are left alone all day with your baby – that's when you realise just how profoundly things have changed. Kate Figes, in her book *Life After Birth*, sums it up:

The books I read . . . spoke in glowing terms about the joys of motherhood without touching on the darker, more frightening areas – the shock of childbirth and the sudden responsibility for a helpless child; the rush of undiluted emotions of love, anxiety, fear, resentment and sometimes hate; the way that relationships with friends, family and the father of the child can change so quickly and so radically; the way that the exhaustion of new motherhood rocks you to the core.

A NEW LIFESTYLE

Although some fathers do take a career break to care for their children, in most families it is the woman who takes on the main task of caring for the baby. Even if you plan to return to work, for the time being you will be spending far more time than usual at home. Even when you do go back to work, the experience won't be the same as it was before, because there is now your child to think about, as well. Wenda, mother of 3-month-old Amy, says:

I've realised now that Amy will always be somewhere in my mind until she's an adult herself. Whatever I'm doing, I still have to make provision for her, but it's not just that. Emotionally she is a part of me now, and when I'm away from her I still wonder what she's doing, and look forward to seeing her. I can't be totally self-centred ever again.

That is the crux of it. Before children, you can, up to a point, please yourself. After children, you quickly learn that for an easy life, you need to put their needs first, especially when they are tiny. It might suit you to go to the supermarket at 2pm, before the afternoon rush. But if that's when your baby usually has a nap, you'd better wait until 4pm – unless that's when she has a feed, in which case fit it in in the morning – unless that's when the health visitor is coming, in which case – oh well, who needs food anyway?

Juggling a baby's demands with your own needs is all part of gradually taking on the new identity, as 'Mummy'. The path towards feeling truly at ease in this role can be a long one. One mother of eight-year-old twins says:

I know it sounds ridiculous, but I have only just fully come to terms with the idea that I am their mother, and I am responsible for their growing up. Until very recently, part of me always felt separate from them – I was clinging on to the old, free me.

Think about it

Part of the difficulty in making the switch from 'free me' to 'Mummy' is that being a mother encompasses so much. Included in the job spec are: comforting, nurturing, giving hands-on care from nappy-changing to bathing, guarding against danger, teaching, loving, helping, accepting, understanding. Oh, and doing all this whilst not losing your temper. It's a great deal to ask.

The world becomes very dangerous

One of the unexpected effects of becoming a mother is the horrible discovery that the world is fraught with danger. Looking after a fragile, vulnerable baby gives you a heightened awareness of the perils that lurk out in the high street. Gill, mother of three-month-old Louisa, says:

I sometimes lie awake at night and imagine juggernauts losing control and mounting the pavement just as I'm walking past with the buggy. I hate going in the car now, in case we have a crash. And I just cannot watch the evening news – the sight of children suffering in any way is too upsetting.

In some ways, being in touch with the dark side of the world is a good thing. Some women go on to try and right some of the wrongs done to children, and many become more prepared to act if they see a child being badly treated. But it can be exhausting and distressing to live in a state of fear. Fortunately, the sense of danger does diminish as children get older, although it never completely goes away.

'No one said it would be boring'

Looking after small children can be dull. No matter how delightful your child, the repetition – 'Do it again, *again*' –

so beloved of small children can be mind-numbing. The practical tasks can also become tedious: putting on the mittens, putting on the socks, finding the shoes, buckling them, putting the mittens on again, finding your cash, keys, coat; organising a drink, nappy, toys, blanket. Just getting out the front door can take half an hour.

Slowing down, if you've been used to a varied, stimulating life, mixing with friends and colleagues in the workplace, can be hard.

Try this

- Talk to other mothers in the same boat. Keep in touch with others from your antenatal class, or look out for music groups, story sessions and any other child-orientated activity where you might meet people.

- If organised groups are not your thing, try to get out every day and go where other parents go – playgrounds, parks, swimming pools.

- Focus on the enjoyment that your baby gives you, rather than on the frustrations of the job.

- Get some time to yourself. A couple of hours one afternoon, an evening once a week. Use whatever care you can squeeze from friends and family to do something just for yourself.

- Remind yourself that you are learning valuable skills. Looking after little children requires organisation, patience, dexterity, creativity and a sense of humour. All of these are useful attributes and you will be glad you have them in years to come. This time is not being wasted.

- Caring for small children does not suit everyone. Don't be afraid to reverse a decision to give up work completely. A part-time job can satisfy your needs and still leave plenty of time for mothering. More on work in Chapter 12, page 118.

WHO AM I?

Some women find a true sense of identity for the first time when they become mothers. Sharon, mother of Jack aged six months, says:

I'd been working in the local building society since I left school and I was bored stiff. I love being at home, knowing that Jack needs me. We have a nice routine together. We go out every day and I feel really satisfied with what I'm doing for the first time ever.

Linda Connell works with PIPPIN, an organisation that trains midwives and health visitors to support couples through a research-backed training programme that is offered to new and expectant parents (see page 218 for details). Linda says:

Sometimes women feel that far from gaining a new identity, they have lost their separate identity. If you ask a man 'Who are you?' he will say he's a solicitor, or a lorry driver – he will identify himself by his occupation. Ask a woman the same question, and she'll usually identify herself as someone's mother, or wife, or partner – she sees herself in terms of relationships with other people, not as a separate individual in her own right.

Tamsin, mother of 4-month-old Cora, explains the feeling.

If you asked me to fill in a form and put my occupation I wouldn't know what to put. I'm a mother, but I don't think of myself as a mother. I don't think I'm maternal. I love Cora, but I'm not totally occupied with her and I don't regard this as the thing I want to do most in life and that I have now finished. I think I'm far too young to give up the ghost.

_____ **Try this** _____

- Make contact with people outside the family, who are in no way connected with you as a mother. An evening class, reading group, exercise class, drama or music group – try anything which does not revolve around children.

- If you are planning to get back into your career, stay in touch with what is going on in your field. Read professional journals, go to meetings and keep in touch with former colleagues.

- Spend time with your partner without the baby. More on how to manage this in Chapter 14, page 141.

_____ **In brief** _____

- It's tough, but once you're a mum, your own needs go to the bottom of the heap for a while.

- Talk to other mothers – they're all in the same boat, and it doesn't seem so bad once you know you're not alone.

- Whether you're fulfilled or frustrated, squeezing some time for yourself into each week can improve your experience of motherhood.

Chapter 8

WHAT'S IT LIKE TO BE A FATHER?

I saved up my holiday and took two weeks leave when Savannah was born. Going back when she was only ten days old was so tough. I didn't want to leave her and my wife for five minutes, never mind a whole day. More than once I skived off work early just so as to get back and give her a bath, or do her evening bottle. Yes, it can be a slog. But it's the best slog in the world. Andy

Becoming a father can change a man's life dramatically, if he lets it. Most fathers do far more hands-on childcare and have closer relationships with their children than was usual for their own father's generation. Everyone stands to benefit from this greater involvement, but taking on the role of active parent, combined with breadwinner, even when one or both of these roles is shared with a partner, calls for a shift in priorities that can be hard.

BEATING THE TIME BANDITS

Time. There's never enough of it. Over 80 per cent of British fathers are working full-time, averaging a gruelling 46-hour week. Weekend working is increasingly common. Paid paternity leave won't be on offer in the UK until 2003, and even then will only cover the first two weeks of a baby's life. Many men find themselves torn between the desire to spend more time with their children, and the need to spend a lot of time at work.

Adrienne Burgess, in her book *Fatherhood Reclaimed*, reveals that, faced with the prevailing ethos of long working hours, fathers develop cunning strategies to buck the system.

They park in the back lot so they won't be seen leaving early, or say they're going to 'another meeting', without saying that it's a meeting with their children.

It's a sad reflection on society's attitudes that men have to resort to underhand tactics to squeeze a few hours of family time into their working lives. Flexible, family-friendly working conditions, though not unheard of, have yet to become widespread. Adrienne Burgess does see some hope on the horizon:

The best present you could give a British father would be truly flexible working, and that doesn't just mean being able to come in half an hour late or leave half an hour early. Many men are keen for this and are sure that their companies would benefit if they worked flexibly. In the long term, enabling both men and women to balance the needs of work and family will entail a revolution in working time, but this may be the revolution that is coming.

The message perhaps is, lobby your employer as much as you can, squeeze the system where you can and don't give up.

HOW MUCH CARING DO DADS DO?

Well over three-quarters of fathers regularly do some of the bathing, feeding, changing and, as children get older, playing and entertaining. Men no longer want to be seen just as financial providers, but as being directly involved with the upbringing and care of their children. This is a huge change in what society expects of a father.

Barry, 48, had two children in his early twenties and then, having divorced and remarried, had two more in his forties.

I don't remember changing a single nappy when my first two were babies. I never pushed the pram – you just didn't. My wife gave up work without even questioning it, and I expected to provide for us all. I worked long hours and when I got home the children were in bed and my dinner was on the table. With my second family, I've been involved right from the start. I've changed nappies, bathed them, walked up and down with them screaming on my shoulder. I've taken them out, not just in the pram, but in the papoose and no one has given me a second glance. It's been wonderful to be so involved – I've enjoyed having these two children so much more than I was able to enjoy my first two, and feel I know them far better.

One reason for this turnaround is the huge rise in the number of women who return to work before their children go to school. Fathers are needed, and some even give up their own jobs for a while to look after the children full-time.

Andrew Tyler is a Relate counsellor who gave up his job for five years to look after his young children while his wife returned to work.

As a man it was a cushy number because my wife would come home from work at 5.30 and I would hand the baby over and could just forget about her within a moment. That is totally different from a woman's experience. I think the nature of the bond is different. I was very connected with both babies, and it was very intimate. Having those deep blue baby eyes looking into your eyes – that was amazing. But I could also separate from them with no trouble. When I wasn't actually looking after them, I could get on with whatever I was doing without thinking about them at all.

WORRIES ABOUT BEING A DAD

Suddenly finding yourself with a small child to care for – and, perhaps for a time also acting as sole supporter of a family of three – can be scary. Parenthood rouses all sorts of mixed emotions, in men and women alike. The trouble for men is that many still find it hard to admit to problems or fears. The old 'macho' image hasn't yet lain down and died, and the need to appear strong and in control means that just owning up to a worry is hard enough, and finding a way to cope with it is even harder.

Men's anxieties

John Lewing is a PIPPIN trainer who has been involved with the Investing in Fathers Project, which was set up to identify and support the needs of young fathers who are not living with their baby's mother. He has talked to dozens of fathers about their experiences. These are just some of the anxieties they have had.

- How will I live up to my partner's and other people's expectations of me as a father?
- My own dad was a lousy father – I'm afraid of ending up like him and treating my own children the same way.
- How will we cope when my partner stops work? Suppose I lose my job, or don't get that promotion?
- I never seem to see the baby because I'm always at work. How can I get to spend more time being part of the family, and still earn enough for us to manage on?
- My partner is totally wrapped up in the baby – am I ever going to get her back?

Identifying problems is only the first step. Where women often turn to friends, family or their partner, men tend not to have the same support systems. PIPPIN research has shown that men are more likely to turn to their partners for support than anyone else. Even so, it may be the woman who has to initiate the conversation – and she can only do this if a man lets on that something's bothering him.

Asking how men can cope with becoming a father is the $64,000 question. My personal opinion is that men do need support, but asking anyone else for help feels totally alien. When a man has problem, he usually goes 'back to his cave' to think it out. A lot of the time this works, as it has done for thousands of years, and when he's thought things through he emerges. When he can't find a solution, it can be really useful if he seeks out another man, one who knows how to listen properly, who can let him talk and help him to move on. Men, if they are lucky, have one male friend who they can share their emotions with. That friend holds the key if a guy is stuck and cannot work things out for himself. John Lewing

But I don't want to grow up

Lots of couples find that the experience of parenting brings them closer together and enriches their relationship. If one partner is unwilling to take on the responsibilities of parenthood, however, much conflict can arise.

Wesley and Louise had been together for two years when Leo was born. Instead of adapting to his new role as father, Wesley took refuge with his model cars. Every evening, he went straight up to the attic and worked on his layout, ignoring Louise's pleas for him to come down and help with the baby. He just couldn't face the responsibility. Louise went for Relate counselling, but Wesley refused to go with her, and after several months, completely exasperated, she left him.

A few months later, however, they got back together, on condition that the model cars were sold. While they were apart, Wesley had realised just what the family did mean to him, and that a live baby, with all its problems and demands, was preferable to playthings. Their counsellor says:

I have heard so many women say that although their part-
ner may be a dad now, he still goes out clubbing/drinking or
whatever. These couples have to try hard to come to a com-
promise, and sometimes the woman has no choice but to
accept that she will bear the brunt of the responsibility for the
children. For some, the only alternative is separation, if the
man simply refuses to change his behaviour.

WHY FATHERS ARE SO IMPORTANT

Men need to know just how important they are to their partner and their child. Adrienne Burgess cites a mass of research showing the benefits of involved and affectionate fathering, for instance:

- Women whose partners are involved fathers are more satisfied with their marriages and are less likely to suffer from postnatal depression.
- There is a clear connection between involved fathering and the happiness and stability of the parents' marriage in mid-life.
- First-borns who have good relationships with their fathers are more accepting of a new sibling.
- Adolescents with good relationships with their fathers have fewer behaviour problems in school or are more self-directed, cheerful and happy.

The list goes on and on. Quite clearly, it is overwhelmingly worthwhile for fathers to take as active a role as possible in the family. Sure, settling down into the role of father takes time. Balancing the different demands means life is busier than it's ever been. But the rewards for men, and for their families, are tremendous. Seize them.

—————————————— **In brief** ——————————————

- Try to cut down on long hours at work.
- Men can do most of the babycare jobs just as well as women can.
- Being a father is a big responsibility. Give yourself time to adjust.
- Dads are really important to the family – don't forget it.

Chapter 9
FAMILY LIFE

I know Rod feels neglected, because I'm so tired. He comes home and I collapse: I don't feel like staying up late talking, or watching tv; which I always used to do. And he doesn't play with the baby enough. When he comes in and the baby's there I say, Look, see what he can do now, and he has a quick look, then goes back to reading his book. Even though we love each other, he feels that he's not very involved and I feel that I don't make him happy any more. Tania, mother of baby aged two months

When you have a child, although you are parents by definition from day one, it can take quite a while before you actually *feel* like parents. Becoming a family sparks off a chain reaction that can have lingering effects on the couple's relationship, which may itself take a nosedive in the months following the birth. Relate counsellors report that couples who come to them with long-term problems frequently identify their difficulties as having started after their first child was born.

WHEN TWO BECOME THREE

Parenthood starts here, for real. No more cosy couple evenings, no more uninterrupted meals and sharing of the day, no more freedom to go to the movies at the drop of a hat. Two have become three and nothing will be the same again.

The Family Triangle

The diagram below shows how the arrival of a baby creates a triangular family relationship, with a range of potential conflicts.

The Family Triangle

A: The couple's relationship, before the birth of their baby.
B: The mother is strongly bonded with her baby, and also closely connected to the father.
C: Both parents are connected to the baby, and are once again strongly linked together.
D: The couple are close, but the baby is out on a limb.
E: Mother and baby are well-bonded, but the father is being excluded.
F: Father and child have the strongest connection, while the mother is being neglected.

When there are just two of you, as in A, you can sort out compromises between yourselves – it's simple. After a baby arrives, the relationship might initially look like B. There is a bond between both parents, and between the father and the baby, but mother and child are particularly intensely connected. It can be hard for the father to start sharing the woman with the baby, but he may only have to relinquish her for a short while. After a few months the pattern will start to look more like C, where the couple's bond has reasserted itself, and both are also connected to the baby.

Sometimes the triangle takes on a different shape. In D, the couple have retained their closeness, but the baby is being left out. This can happen when a child arrives after a couple have already been together for many years and they are unable – or unwilling – to let the baby intrude on their togetherness. In E, the mother is closely bonded to the baby, but the father is excluded. This happens when the close mother/baby bond of the initial weeks doesn't loosen up to allow the father back in, or when the parents' relationship was rocky before the baby arrived. In F, the father is strongly connected to the baby but the mother feels left out.

With all these configurations, dangers arise when the reshuffle of family relationships establishes a pattern that develops into a permanent rift between the couple.

───────────── **Think about it** ─────────────

- Which of the diagrams best fits your family? Go for your intuitive answer.

- What might that mean for the people involved?

- How would you like your family triangle to look?

The pain of exclusion

Women often turn to their own mothers for support and help when a baby arrives, and here a different sort of triangle can be set up, where three adults are competing over the baby. Blessed the mother or mother-in-law who knows how to keep the right amount of distance.

Colin and Jackie came for counselling because their relationship was at rock bottom, six months after their baby's birth. Jackie's mother came every day to help with the baby while Colin was at work, and this led to constant rows.

Colin, after several sessions of counselling, began to realise that he had felt pushed out of his own family at the age of 9, when he was sent away to boarding school. Twenty-five years later, when he walked out of the front door every morning as his mother-in-law walked in, all those old feelings of being excluded, and unwanted, came flooding back. Ultimately, mother-in-law had to step back, but it wasn't easy. Deep-seated jealousy can be a very difficult problem, and is an area where professional counselling may be helpful.

--------------- **Think about it** ---------------

- Is someone feeling left out in your family group?

- Is someone intruding into your family set-up? How can you tackle this?

- Has something happened in the past to make the feelings especially painful?

WHAT ABOUT US?

Things become even more complicated if this is not your first child, or you introduce a new baby into a stepfamily.

Helping older children to accept a new baby

In most families there is a gap of between one and three years between children, which means that a toddler who is used to being the centre of attention has to accept competition from a new baby. Even if your children are older, they will still have to adapt to the fact that you simply have less time for them than you did, even if they don't see the new baby as a rival.

—————————————— **Try this** ——————————————

- Talk to children about the new baby well before its arrival. Involve them in thinking about names, bedrooms and so on.

- Whenever possible, arrange things so that while one of you takes care of the baby, the other gives the older children their full attention.

- Arrange for the baby to 'give' a small present to its brothers or sisters when it arrives.

- Get visitors to pay attention to your other children first, before making a bee-line for the baby.

- Let your children cuddle and touch the new baby. Try not to whip the newborn away every time a child wants to touch it – keep a protective eye open, but don't over-react.

Introducing a new baby into a stepfamily

Babies are powerful stimulators of emotion, and never more so than in a stepfamily, where feelings may already be stretched. On the negative side, a baby can make existing children feel jealous, or afraid of being sidelined as they see their parent's love for a new child. Ex-spouses may also feel resentful or angry over their former partner's happiness. On a more positive note, a new baby can form an important central link in a family, being related in some way to everybody. And a new baby demonstrates that the new family is stable and permanent.

Think about it

- Be aware that children who do not live with you may feel they are no longer wanted, now there is a new baby. Parents should reassure them, and give extra time and love. Step-parents can help ensure stepchildren form a relationship with their new half-sibling.

- Try to share out the love – don't let the new child become the spoilt focus of everyone's attention. Equally, don't lavish so much attention on the other children that you neglect the needs of the newest member of the family.

- Do not expect the new child automatically to enhance or strengthen existing relationships within the stepfamily. If you are lucky, this will happen by itself in time. It places a great burden on a child if he realises that he has failed to make the family happy.

BECOMING ADOPTIVE PARENTS

If the transition to parenthood comes as something of a shock, even when you've had nine months to get used to the idea, it can be even more devastating if you are suddenly presented with a child with very little warning. This happened to Caroline and Bill, whose story began on page 32.

Our daughter was three when she came to us, and we had just three weeks from first being told about her, to her moving in. We had met her and spent time with her over those weeks, but it was still quite a shock to bring her home. Several years later we adopted another child, this time a baby, and we had just one week to prepare ourselves for his arrival.

The whole thing was pretty breathtaking – the speed with which it all happened. One day I was working, the next I was on maternity leave – fortunately the company I worked for offered leave to adoptive parents, otherwise I don't know how we would have coped. When you adopt a child, particularly one who isn't a baby, they take a lot of settling in, they need loads of time. It wasn't until the three-year-old was almost four and things were getting easier that I realised just how hard it had been. One problem was that she didn't love us at first, and nor did we love her. It took time for that bond to form, and it was about nine months before we really felt like parents.

The change to our lifestyle took some getting used to. We'd never fought much before, but we started rowing about how to handle her, and about setting up routines we'd never needed before, like mealtimes and bedtimes. It was very stressful to be arguing like that instead of enjoying a blissful time of shared parenthood together. It takes time to settle down as a family and for all the new relationships to become established. The whole experience of adopting was a huge challenge to our relationship. We've never regretted it, but at times it has been a struggle.

DREAMS V. REALITY

Parenthood is greatly romanticised in adverts and magazines, and there is a taboo about telling it like it is.

The baby balance sheet

Most people find that their children bring greater fulfilment than they ever dreamed possible. That is the plus of having children – the joy and delight they bring in so many unlooked-for ways is immense. But, like all of life's big experiences, there are no gains without losses. Many of the losses brought about by having a child are felt most acutely

during the first year or so. After that, parents gradually settle down into their new way of life and some of the things
that were lost start to be regained. These are some losses
and gains identified by new parents, when their babies were
around eight weeks old.

Losses	Gains
Stella: *The freedom to come and go as I please.*	*The pleasure of drifting at home, with none of the pressures of work*
Andy: *Sex!*	*The satisfaction of caring for Savannah and seeing her thrive.*
Shipra: *My identity as a working person, plus the friends I had at work and the fun of being there.*	*It's lovely to be a parent with my partner – it really has strengthened the bond between us.*
Natalie: *I used to be slender, but now I've got enormous breasts and a belly to match.*	*I feel more grown up now, as if I've finally joined the ranks of the adults.*

Losses like these, even when they are partially balanced by
gains, could put a lot of pressure on your relationship.
Change is seldom comfortable, and it can be tempting to
ignore the strains and muddle on as best you can, even if
you're aware that having a baby is not always the idyllic
experience you'd imagined. It's harder, but far better, to face
up to the problems and try to sort them out.

Facing problems

One of the difficult truths of having children is that
they do intervene in your relationship. It can be so, so

easy to put your own relationship on the back burner during the intensely demanding early days – and leave it there.

The fact is, though, that the wellbeing of your relationship is hugely important, both to you and to your children. It isn't selfish or indulgent to take time for yourselves – it's essential, even if your relationship is fundamentally strong. And if the baby's arrival has put your relationship on the skids, finding time now to address the problems is crucial. Counsellor Lucy Selleck says:

Don't shelve problems – there's never a perfect time to tackle them, so tackle them now. So many people come to me saying, 'We couldn't do anything about our problems – we were too busy. We had one baby, then another . . .' In twenty years time you could be getting divorced because you let the children take up all your time, and left your problems unresolved, and now there's nothing left.

If having a baby seems to have caused big ripples in your relationship, don't let those resentments build up. Try to talk them through without blaming, or getting angry. Don't assume you know what your partner is feeling.

Talking about relationship problems is never easy. One way to try and open up the subject is to use uninterrupted listening. Bill and Katy went on a PIPPIN training course (see page 218) where they learned this technique, described overleaf, in order to break their cycle of saying nothing, then finally exploding into a giant row.

Rather than getting all steamed up about a situation, you can sit down with your partner who listens to what you're saying without interrupting. I found that very, very useful. It's got to be better than shouting your head off. Bill

_____ **Try this** _____

- Agree on a time. It needn't be long, but choose a moment that suits you both, when you're not hungry or especially tired.

- Take turns and listen to each other, uninterrupted, for a certain amount of time. One of you might talk for five or ten minutes about any particular problems and anxieties, while the other listens carefully without interrupting. Then the other partner has an equal amount of time to do the same.

- It is very important not to use language that blames or criticises the other. The object is not to attack or undermine each other, but to try and understand what the problems are. Say, 'I feel abandoned when you go to the pub after work instead of coming home to me and the baby', rather than, 'I'm furious that you spend so much time at the pub. You've never bothered to come home on time, and since we've had the baby things have got even worse.'

- When you have heard each other, go away and think about what has been said. Your first reactions may be 'hot' thoughts – anger, resentment. You might feel like crying. Let these feelings pass, and focus on what your partner actually said, so that you end up with a clearer understanding of his or her feelings. Then, when you're ready, use your new insights to talk the problem through again calmly. Try to move towards a solution that satisfies you both.

_____

If you find this sort of listening exercise extremely difficult, or even impossible – and many couples do – someone outside your relationship, such a counsellor, might be able to help you unravel your feelings more easily.

_____ **In brief** _____

- Family life is different from couple life. Expect it to change, and you won't be disappointed.

- Other children in the family will also feel a difference when a new baby arrives.

- There's precious little romance about parenthood. A lot of it is hard graft – but there are huge rewards.

- Be aware of problems. Like weeds, they can smother a good relationship almost before you notice they're there.

Chapter 10

WE'RE IN THIS TOGETHER

I was so nasty to Scott, he was nervous of talking to me. He found it hard to feel part of the family thing – he'd never held a baby before Amy was born. He'd try to do things and I'd be telling him to do it my way. And I was feeling down: the perfect mother doesn't feel like that, so you put on this pretence, saying, 'I'm fine,' when at times you think the day is never going to end. Now I know, but at the time I thought, We're never going to get over this, we've ruined our life. Keri

Relationships come under stress when a baby is born. Research shows that at least two-thirds of new parents find the first few months an uphill struggle, regardless of how thrilled they are with their new offspring.

BE PREPARED

So what's it like, what's it *really* like, having a new baby? One thing's certain – everything will seem different from how it was before. Susan Maushart, author of *The Mask of Motherhood* says:

After you've had a baby, your body will never, ever be the same again. Nor will your mind. Or your heart. Having kids changes women in different ways, but it changes all of us. Parenthood forces us to grow, stretching us in new and uncomfortable directions and teaching us lessons we never wanted to learn.

Change of any sort forces you to re-draw your mental 'map' of how your life looks. Before the baby, if the couple's relationship is close, their mental maps will feature each other in prominent positions. Once a baby arrives, the baby will be at the forefront of the mother's map and probably the father's too. Other major concerns such as work, other family members and so on, have to jostle for new, maybe less dominant positions. This mental realignment takes time, and can be destabilising and painful.

Feelings about parenthood

The experience of parenthood may be quite different from what you'd dreamed of. Research has shown that only four sets of parents out of every hundred find that child rearing lives up to their expectations, while almost half of all new parents would have delayed having children if they'd known what it was really going to be like.

Parenthood and babycare are hugely glamorised in the press and media. Flip through any magazine, or switch on the TV and watch the images of slender, smiling mothers; energetic, handsome fathers; charmingly chubby, squeaky-clean, gurgling babies. With this kind of image bombarding us from all sides, it can be quite a shock when the reality doesn't match.

—————————————— **Try this** ——————————————

If you are reading this book before your baby is born, make a list of your expectations about what life will be like when the baby arrives. Get your partner to do the same. Think about how you will look and feel, how the baby will behave, how you'll be coping with parenthood, how your sex life will fare, how you'll deal with your finances – anything that strikes you. Go through the lists together and see how far you agree. Talk about what the reality might be like. Try to be as realistic as you can.

Put the list away, and look at it again together, when the baby is a few months old. What things are better than you'd anticipated? Which are worse? How realistic were your ideas?

CARING FOR YOUR BABY TOGETHER

There's a lot to learn with a new baby. Getting good, up-to-date information can make a big difference to how well you feel in control. Books are the most important source of information, but there's also plenty of help around in magazines and leaflets, and on TV, radio and the Internet. People who've experienced what you're going through can be a great source of information and provide support and reassurance. Pick the brains of friends, colleagues, family. The majority of men get most of their information from their partner, relying on her to do the reading and talking. One first-time father told Fathers Direct:

There's been a few things on telly lately which have been pretty good. I get most of the info from the missus and she gets books out of the library. We get stuff from all over but mainly I rely on the missus.

In the end though, the best that books can do is give a broad outline. Every baby is an individual, and no publication can tell you exactly how you or your child will respond in any situation. A mother with a four-week-old baby who refused to nap during the day, and slept only intermittently at night, writes:

Have been searching the baby book for help, and despairing. It says, '. . . the baby settles to sleep contentedly after every feed . . . If you are clever you need never be woken more than once in the night.' Ha! That author is talking out of the back of her neck (or worse).

Men and parenting

More and more men are becoming actively involved in the care of their children. Even so, men may have been brought up in a family where men were not expected to be so close to their children, or might believe that it is the woman's role to do the parenting, while they act as breadwinner. Becoming a parent can bring out entrenched ideas of traditional roles, which can be hard to break.

_____ **Try this** _____

There are lots of ways men can become close to their babies and children. These suggestions come from fathers who've already been there.

- Don't treat babycare as a chore, but use it as a chance to get to know your baby.

- Talk and play with your baby while you change nappies or give them a bath. They'll soon learn to recognise you, and give you a lovely gummy beam every time they see you.

- If your partner is breastfeeding, you can still do the burping after a feed, change and bath, or settle the baby to sleep.

- Don't worry if you feel as if you'll never get the hang of
  it. Looking after a baby takes practice, and if your partner seems better at it than you are, that's just because
  she gets to do it more often.

Beware of becoming territorial

A baby belongs to both its parents. If both of you are going
to have a growing and meaningful relationship with your
child, the sooner you start getting to know him through caring for him, the better. If one of you – often the mother –
decrees that only she can warm bottles, change nappies or
whatever, the other is likely to feel redundant, and will soon
stop offering to help. It is not unusual for women to set
themselves goals of perfection, and to behave as if no one
else has the divine ability to care for their baby.

If mum does all the caring, she's likely to do all the playing, and all the feeding, and all the listening and chatting
and reading as your child grows. Share every aspect of
upbringing right from the start, and you set up patterns
that will last right through childhood, *and* bring everyone
enjoyment and fulfilment. Not only that – if you can rely on
each other to take over, whatever the job that needs to be
done, then both of you can always be sure of getting breaks,
and that can be the most valuable benefit of all.

Many mothers will recognise their difficulty in letting go
of their precious baby. Maya, whose two children are now
aged three and one, recognises the symptoms all too well.

*I've been Lady Madonna, either pregnant or breastfeeding or
both, for four years now. You get into a cycle of perfect effi-
ciency which you think will fall apart if anyone else lays a finger on the child, and there's your poor husband hanging
around saying, 'Um, could I help?' and you're saying, 'No!
You won't do it right!' It's mad. I only stopped when one of*

my sisters said she thought I'd have a nervous breakdown if I carried on trying to do everything myself. I was so shocked that it was visible to her when it wasn't even really visible to me. So I asked Steve, 'Is it true? Is that what's happening to us?' And he said, 'Yes, and we must sort it out.'

Think about it

- If you are reluctant to accept help or to allow your partner to do everyday things for the baby, ask yourself why?

- Even if your partner might not do a job as well or as quickly as you can, is that a reason for excluding him? A few crooked nappies or a bit of soap left behind the ears isn't going to hurt anyone. Prevent your partner from helping now and you may damage your relationship *and* find yourself taking the lion's share of the responsibility for raising your family.

Aim for balance

Gail and Robert came to Relate, because they had completely lost touch with each other. The counsellor asked about their daily routine. Every evening, they devoted themselves to their little son's needs, together. Together, they played with him. Together, they watched as he fed. Together, they bathed him. Together, they lulled him to sleep. Together, they collapsed, speechless from weariness, their own meal unprepared, and fell asleep in opposite armchairs.

The solution? Share the tasks and don't neglect your own needs. If one gives the bath, the other can make a start on a meal. Next night, you can swap. It sounds obvious and if this couple hadn't been so exhausted they would have worked it out for themselves. Tiredness and emotional highs and lows had affected their ability to think clearly and they'd got themselves trapped in a routine that felt unbreakable.

It's important to sort out the way you care for your baby so that both of you feel happy. Not always easy, especially if one is feeling defensive, and the other resentful. Maya, the Lady Madonna whose sister warned her of the dangers looming for her relationship, found it very hard to talk about what was going on. In the end her health visitor offered to act as intermediary and sat in with Maya and Steve to help them talk things over. She did it by being very sensitive and unpushy, while still making sure that each of them got a chance to say what they felt and that the other one heard and acknowledged what was being said.

Some health visitors are trained in this kind of skill. If yours is not, a trusted friend or family member might be able to help, although it is very important that they do not take sides. Or you can talk it through yourselves, without a third party there.

Talk about it

These tips can help you towards more fruitful communcation.

- Pick a good moment, when you are both feeling calm and relaxed.

- Don't call each other names, or take the opportunity to offload all your negative feelings. The aim is to arrive at a good solution for everyone.

- Spell out what you mean. Try to explain why you feel the way you do, and be precise, not vague. 'I feel as if I'm not needed when you stop me from bathing the baby,' is a more helpful starting point than, 'You just want to do everything and you don't care about how I feel.'

- Don't give up. It takes practice to learn to communicate better. Don't expect everything to be solved immediately, but keep at it and bit by bit you will start to see changes.

How to build confidence

At first, a baby's seemingly inexplicable patterns of sleeping and crying can make you feel completely at sea. When you're seized by fears – what if you *can't* stop the crying, suppose the baby's ill, how do you know if she's too hot, too cold, hungry, in pain – turn to each other for support and learn to trust your instincts.

———————————— **Try this** ————————————

Bolster each others' confidence as you gradually get used to caring for the baby. These pointers apply to both partners.

- Showing appreciation helps to build confidence and lets your partner know that you notice what they are doing. You can say, 'What a brilliant bit of nappy-changing,' or 'It was great that you took the baby out while I got on with the supper.'

- Tell your partner when they've done something you particularly appreciate, and describe exactly what it was, so that they can do it again. 'Thanks a lot for making up the formula for tomorrow and getting the bottles into the steriliser. That's an enormous help.' That way they'll feel good because they're giving you what you want, and you feel stroked as well.

- Notice how the baby responds to you both. Look at her with a blank face, and the baby turns away. Talk, smile, sing to the baby and she'll respond. Pull faces and see how the baby mimics you. The more you try to make contact with the baby, the more response you'll get, and the closer you will feel.

BEING A PARENT IN A STEPFAMILY

Keeping a successful grip on a stepfamily, and still devoting time and energy to your relationship as a couple, takes some doing. A Relate counsellor explains:

Sometimes we see couples in this situation who are so determined to be good parents and keep everyone happy, that they completely neglect themselves. Many people feel guilty because they've had a baby that their other children resent, so they go out of their way to compensate for that by giving in to the older children on everything.

The trouble is that that doesn't help – in fact it makes things worse, because children need boundaries, and feel insecure if they don't know where they stand. It's a question of striking a balance between allowing your kids to express themselves, but then saying, 'I heard you, but this is how it's going to be . . .' and then telling them what your limits are.

Bringing a new baby into a stepfamily certainly makes waves, and it can be quite a while before everything calms down. Remember, though, even when the situation seems so bad that you can't imagine it ever improving, that one thing is certain. Things always change, and they can change for the better as long as you are able to keep on looking at the problems and trying to understand them.

WHAT KIND OF PARENTS DO YOU WANT TO BE?

Becoming a parent inevitably arouses memories of your own childhood. Everyone has ideas, based on their own experiences, good and bad, about what a childhood should be like, and what kind of relationship a loving parent should have with her or his children.

If your childhood was happy and untroubled, you'll want to recreate that for your children. If all or part of your childhood was a hard or miserable time, then you might have a whole list of traps you want to avoid – and at the same time you might fear repeating bad patterns just because they are all you know about parenting. This is what some new parents have to say on the subject:

I don't want my children to have a childhood like mine. My parents didn't know how to show love – I sometimes wonder if they even felt it. I find I'm inhibited already from saying how much I adore my baby – part of me feels it wrong to show that emotion.

My mother was the archetypal earth mother. She didn't have a job and her life was centred on us. It was lovely, but I know I can't do that for my children – life is different now, and I'll be going back to work when the baby is six months old. So I'm not sure what kind of mother figure I'll be for him.

I'm the child of a broken marriage. My mum and dad split up when I was seven. Now my own marriage is in danger of breaking up and my son is only two. I feel that a lot of things that went wrong in my parents' situation happened because they never talked to each other about anything. A lot of my problems now could probably have been avoided if my husband and I had gone into all the deeper issues before we even considered having a child.

My mum had a job right through my childhood, which was pretty unusual at the time. In the school holidays, I was always the one with the sandwich box, being shunted off to someone else's house for the day. It didn't strike me as odd because I was so used to it, and I knew my mum loved me to bits. And now I'm doing just the same with my daughter – always plotting about how I can squeeze a few more hours for me to work.

------------------ **Think about it** ------------------

- Be kind to yourself. You aren't going to be the perfect parent, and nor is anybody else, because the perfect parent does not exist. All you can do is your best, and some days doing your best is much easier than it is on others.

- You can't sort out all your hang-ups about your own childhood before your children are born – and you won't even realise what some of your hang-ups are, until you are a parent.

- Talk to each other about your childhoods, your parents, and your ideas about being a parent. Find out where you agree, and where you differ. Keep talking.

- We often fall into familiar patterns of behaviour, without even realising we are doing it. A partner who knows that you don't want to repeat old patterns can help you nip these tendencies in the bud. Liz describes how her partner did this for her:

  My dad had a foul temper and used to shout at my brother and me. I thought that was normal, and grew up thinking it was OK to yell at people who were annoying you. If I lose my rag with our son, my first reaction is often to shout at him. If my husband is around he just says: 'OK Harold (my dad's name), cool it.' It's more effective than saying the dreaded, 'You sound just like your father,' because it stops me in my tracks and makes me laugh in spite of my anger. And that defuses the whole situation.

Positive thinking

Counsellor Denise Knowles sometimes sees couples who are struggling to be really good parents.

It's true, children can be an enormous drain, but at the same time they give you so much. People sometimes lose sight of the love and laughter that children bring, because they're bogged down by the responsibility. It is a daunting task, but it helps to focus on what you are gaining. Concentrate on the skills and coping strategies that you are learning. Say to yourself, Didn't I handle that well? when you avert a toddler's tantrum, or lull a fretful baby to sleep. If you have adjusted to being a parent, the messages you are handing to your children are going to be handed on to your grandchildren. You are giving your children more than you can imagine. It is so worthwhile.

_____ **In brief** _____

- It's impossible to imagine what having a child is like until you do it.

- Share the care and don't be possessive. The baby belongs to both of you.

- If someone says 'You sound just like your mother', they're probably right – but it is possible to learn new ways of parenting.

PART THREE
PRACTICAL MATTERS

Chapter 11
WHO DOES WHAT?

Sometimes I reckon it's the woman who thinks, Oh, he'll mess it up and won't do it as well as I do. But men can learn, can't they? The first time Efosa put a nappy on the baby, it was falling off her, but now he's a real expert, just as good as I am. Neither of us was born with this knowledge, we've both had to learn. Our problem is that he's just not here to change nappies or do anything else. He doesn't get in until 8pm and she's in bed by then and I'm knackered. But if I waited for him to come in and cook the supper we'd be starved so I do it, and all the other household stuff. When we were both working we used to clean round the house at weekends, but now I'd rather have weekends free to take the baby out, or catch up on some sleep. Everything's different now. Chinwe

The change in domestic balance begins when the woman stops work in late pregnancy. Couples who previously both worked full-time have to renegotiate who does what. Priorities change, as they have done for Chinwe and Efosa. Homes which stayed clean and tidy because no one was there all day, suddenly sprout mess and dirt. Babies take up time, spent in feeding, comforting, playing, taking out, and also in the hard graft of nappy changing, washing, making up bottles and preparing food. Keeping on top of the domestic side of life becomes a whole new ball game.

WHOSE RESPONSIBILITY?

Just whose job is it to vacuum, dust and wash the dishes? Even if you've always shared the responsibility, you may find that now one of you is at home – almost always the woman – there is an expectation that that person will also take on the lion's share of the domestic responsibilities.

It can be hard for the partner who is out all day to realise just what it is like to be at home with a baby. A man may act surprised when he comes home and finds the house still in chaos. Yet a woman's day can easily be filled with time-consuming baby-related tasks, particularly if she is breastfeeding, which in itself can take hours. In what little time remains, she may be too tired to tackle the cleaning, or need a break.

One simple way to demonstrate to a partner who thinks staying at home is a soft option, is to let him experience it for himself, as Steph did:

Went out for a pizza with Sally tonight, first time I have been out by myself in four months – heaven! Nat was going to cook himself a meal, read the paper, all while he was looking after Finn. Came back to find him frazzled – Finn had cried a lot, Nat had only just got his meal when I got back at 10, the paper was unopened and there were toys and stuff scattered everywhere. Think it was a real eye-opener for him, just how fragmented time is once there's a baby around.

Exhaustion plays a part in making the housework seem like an insurmountable chore. Jobs that previously you would have whipped through in minutes without even thinking about it, become a huge burden when you are very tired. Fran, mother of six-month-old Jasper, describes her feelings and her home:

Tiredness is dreadful. Everything seems too much, I feel on the brink of losing control – anything can push me over, any minor irritation. There's so much to do and I've no time or energy. The house gets dirtier and untidier, the houseplants droop, dead flowers wilt in my vases, the garden's completely neglected. We have eaten frozen fish bakes, bunged in the oven from the freezer and tasting of god-knows-what for the last three days. Just a night or two of eight hours sleep would make all this seem easy to cope with. I try so hard to remember that these phases pass. Hang on to that. In a month or two it'll all be different. Please.

Running a home is a demanding job, as is caring for a baby. One recurring problem is that this kind of work is often not perceived as being 'real' work, because it takes place in the home, and is unpaid.

A real job

Women who have been used to the status and independence attached to having a paid job, have to adjust to the role of mother and homemaker – a painful and difficult transition for some. Likewise, men have to get used to the idea of their partner in a new role, and must learn to value her contribution just as much as they valued her salary before. If the woman's new role is undervalued, it can cause serious problems. Maria and Trevor came for counselling because their sex life had dwindled to nothing. The counsellor explained:

Trevor still fancied the pants off Maria, but she was having none of it. The relationship had virtually broken down. Maria was at home, caring for their 18-month baby and three-year-old – a choice they had made together when the first child was born. But because Trevor was out all day working in an office, he seemed to think she had it easy. When he came home and found her tired, he got tetchy. He wanted her to listen to an in-depth account of his day in the office, but when she tried to tell him what had been going on for her at home he dismissed it with, 'Oh, I know all that.'

Over the last year Maria had felt increasingly resentful. Looking after two small children and keeping the house immaculate, as Trevor liked it, was not only wearing her down, it wasn't even being appreciated. There was no com-munication – in fact, no conversation of any sort – between them. Maria longed for an adult conversation about the out-side world, but Trevor only wanted her as a dumping ground for his office-angst, before he crashed out in front of the TV. Given the gulf between them, it was no surprise that the last thing Maria felt like was being a sexual partner.

The counsellor helped them to open up to each other.

At first Trevor felt very criticised and reacted defensively, but with guidance they were able to air their grievances without blaming each other. Once he started really listening and respond-ing to Maria and taking an interest in her life, her anger dim-inished so that she could hear about his day and sympathise with him. They became part of each others' worlds again, as grad-ually he reconnected with the family. And once that happened, Maria was able to take him back as a sexual partner.

The phase of being deeply involved with a young family is relatively short-lived, but it is very intense, and it's very easy to lose sight of each other when you are in the midst of it. By staying in touch with each others' worlds, and valuing the contribution that both of you make to the family, you can stay in touch as partners.

WHO CARES FOR THE BABY?

Men who are working long hours may only see their babies for an hour or so a day, if that. But if men are around more during the day, and at weekends, who does the babycare then?

Suppose your baby produces a truly disgusting nappy-ful, what one father described as 'a knees to armpits job'. Who takes on the clean-up? Nappy changing, particularly dirty-nappy changing, seems to be one area couples often argue about. Says one mother of her husband:

He does change nappies, but he tries to get out of it if it's dirty. Last week he took the baby upstairs to change him and when he got the nappy off it was dirty, so he called me and asked me what to do. He knew, really – he was just hoping that I'd say, OK, I'll do it for you.

Of course, for every father who avoids dirty nappies, there are many who do take them in their stride, know how to work the washing machine and generally are as hands-on as their partners. Most men are willing to be involved in housework, although arriving at a point where both partners see the chores as a joint responsibility isn't always possible. More often, women are seen as being 'in charge' of domestic matters, and men give 'help'.

In the end, however, perhaps it doesn't matter too much how you label these things. Each couple has to work out their own status quo. When you're genuinely happy with the balance of responsibility, however it falls, then there's no problem. If someone is feeling hard done by and resentful, then it matters.

SHIFTING THE BALANCE

Things can change again, if a woman goes back to work either full or part-time after a few months. Interestingly, research shows that the domestic balance may not alter to take account of her additional workload. Women who work outside the home also do more hours of housework than their partners. Counsellor Lucy Selleck says that problems set in when couples ignore change.

Often the woman has always done most of the housework, and even though time has moved on, and she has less and less time with children and maybe a job to contend with as well, the routine is that she does it, and so she continues to do it. That said, women often complain to me that their partners don't do enough in the house, but I point out that the women have to take some responsibility for that situation. If you're feeling overloaded, say something. Men aren't mindreaders. Don't harbour resentment for months and then end up shouting, but tackle the subject calmly and reasonably.

Try this

- Discuss the way the work is shared out and try to agree on how you will do it in future.

- Don't take refuge in silently punishing your partner for not doing their fair share. Grasp the nettle and tell them how your feel. Beth says:

    When your partner isn't pulling their weight in the family, you stop going the extra mile. So if you're in the supermarket and would normally buy their favourite cheese or whatever as a treat, you stop doing that. It's petty, but you think, Why should I? What have you done to deserve it? You get irritated when they promise to mend the fence or paint the skirting board, then never get round to it. You start to see just the faults and resentment can grow quickly if the root cause isn't addressed.

- A reasonable, non-blaming approach, is far more likely to get the results you want than a prolonged rant, or endless nagging. Don't end the discussion until you have come up with a plan of action.

- Keep on asking, so that sharing the load becomes a normal and accepted part of family life.
- Take on the jobs that you prefer. If one of you loves cooking, fine, let the other shop instead. If you both hate ironing, take it in turns. Decide together who is going to do what job.
- If you have older children, include them in the household routine. Even quite small children can drop their dirty clothes into the wash basket, take their plate over to the sink or shake up their duvets and pillows every morning.

MAKING LIFE EASIER

Juggling home, job and family takes skill and organisation. Some people love lists and rotas, while others can't stand them, and are better off sorting things as they occur.

Do rotas work?

They can be very helpful, especially if kept simple and informal. Jot the details on your calendar, if you want a reminder.

- Set up rotas together, and get everyone's agreement to the jobs they are down for. One reason why rotas 'slip' after a week or two, and all the tasks gravitate back to the woman, is that she often sets up the rota without referring to anyone else.
- Swap the jobs around to make it more interesting – going to the supermarket is less of a drag if you don't do it week in, week out.

Lighten the load

Domestic jobs have to be done, but there are ways to make them less arduous. Unfortunately, all these suggestions cost money but many families find it worthwhile to budget them in, for the sake of not getting overloaded.

- Pay someone to do an hour or two of cleaning for you every week, or farm out the ironing.
- Invest in a dishwasher, tumble drier, larger fridge and a freezer and microwave.
- Use more ready-prepared food. Keep one or two ready-meals in the freezer for those nights when you just don't have energy to cook.
- Find out if your supermarket delivers. You may be able to put in an order via the Internet, or over the phone, and save yourself hours of tedious shelf-trawling.

SAY GOODBYE TO GUILT

It's easy to get caught up in feeling that you must do everything to perfection. Learning to lower your standards, just a little, can free up precious time that you can spend enjoying your family. 'Women get raddled with guilt at failing to cope and then get defensive because they also feel guilty about asking for help,' says Lucy Selleck, who offers this advice:

- Set boundaries and make it clear just what you can and cannot do.
- Work out a fair system that leaves both of you feeling OK about how much you are both doing.
- Don't be afraid to break the mould and step out of your old roles. It can be very refreshing and liberating to change things, and you have nothing to lose.
- Don't be afraid to ask for help. Remember people need to know what their partners want if they are to help them effectively.
- Sit down together and talk about your needs, then discuss how best to meet them.

In brief

- Be prepared for disagreements, when it comes to sorting out who does what in the house.

- Value each others' roles – at home, or at work, both parents are equally important.

- Lower your standards, if that's what it takes to get on top of the domestic side of life.

Chapter 12

WORKING STRATEGIES

Before you have a baby you have no idea just how much your life is going to change. I'm a freelance editor and I thought I'd be able to work while the baby was sleeping to start with, and then later have someone in for a few hours a day to take care of him while I worked. When it came to it, Elliott hardly slept during the day, so I had to delay my return to work. I got a childminder who came to the house but it was impossible to concentrate, because every time I heard a wail I went rushing out to see what was wrong. So now I take him to a nursery three mornings a week and I come home to work. Abby, mother of Elliott aged ten months

Almost two in every three mothers of preschool children goes to work. For many women, the return to work is driven by financial need – they just can't afford to stay at home, even if they'd like to. For others the need is a personal one: they don't want to quit their place on the career ladder, they enjoy their jobs and need to be doing them in order to be happy.

THE IMPACT OF WORK ON YOUR RELATIONSHIP

When you're deciding on the best plan for your future at work, think about money and career prospects, yes, but don't forget the impact that your decisions will make on your relationship with your partner.

Working once you have children means embarking on a juggling act, trying to balance everything so that you get enough of work, while you and your child, and you and your partner, get enough of each other. Not easy.

Having a baby has a knock-on effect on the rest of your lives. The choices you and your partner make about the who, what and when of returning to work, will affect you both, well into the future.

Carly was in the middle of studying when she got pregnant and had to rethink her plans. She wrote:

Talked to my tutor and she said I could go on and teach, or do some more studying, or some counselling – lots of options. Later I was telling Dan about this. 'Hmmm,' he said, 'it would be hard work doing all that, and looking after the baby, and looking after me. I like my seafood lasagnes' (I made one on Sunday while he was decorating). Is there a fear in him that I'll fill my life with so much that there won't be room for him? Must admit, I can't see how I could possibly do everything, especially once there's a baby. But I'm going to try.

_____ **Talk about it** _____

- If a potential conflict arises, as it did for Carly and Dan, don't ignore it. The best solutions are those that go as far as possible towards meeting everyone's needs.

- Keep an open mind. What struck you both as being the perfect solution before the event, may need some fine-tuning once you're doing it for real.

- Lack of money, lack of time, too much domestic or baby-care stuff to do – all these can put a strain on your relationship. Be realistic about how much you can both do without getting worn out, and look for workable solutions.

WAYS OF WORKING

In most families, it's the woman who both takes on much of the day-to-day childcare, and makes the most radical changes in her working life. Deciding on these changes isn't always easy. Kate Figes, in *Life After Birth*, points out:

For many women motherhood brings a welcome breathing space to a boring job or an opportunity to give up work completely for a while. For others, motherhood raises intense and sometimes overwhelming feelings of inner conflict and phenomenal guilt about their working life.

Mothers returning to work full-time

Things may slowly be changing, but many women returning to work after maternity leave find that few concessions are made to their new responsibilities. An arduous and inflexible job can put a huge strain on your home life but it can be a good solution for some women. Marie-Louise, a graphic designer and mother of two-year-old twins, says:

Going back to work takes away the anxiety of where the money's coming from. I'd rather not do it, but at least my employers are flexible and as long as the work is done they don't mind how I organise my hours.

Research carried out by the University of Bristol on a group of over 500 mothers found that within two years of returning full-time more than a third had either switched to part-time work, or had given up work altogether. Look at the following questions, and talk the answers over with your partner before committing to full-time work.

_____ **Think about it** _____

- Does your company demand long or unsociable hours?

- Are they likely to offer the flexibility to cope with crises such as a sick child?

- Is there prejudice within the company – open or, more probably, unspoken – against working mothers?

- Are you fit, and do you tire easily? Full-time work combined with motherhood requires stamina.

- Will the values promoted by your job 'chime' with your new values as a parent? One woman who worked in the fashion industry says:

  I used to love my job, but now I've got a baby, clothes, and what we all ought to be wearing, just don't seem so important any more.

- Are you and your partner both happy about leaving your child with someone else for the greater part of the day?

Fathers working full-time

Men's careers aren't generally disrupted to the same extent as women's when a baby is born, but even so their working patterns may change.

_____ **Think about it** _____

- Broken nights can make you tired in the first few months, and you may feel that you are underperforming at work. Be easy on yourself – you can only do so much.

- Try to reduce your hours at work so that you can see your baby every day. Drop the after-work drink, and cut down on long lunchbreaks so that you can get away sooner.

- Find out how flexible your employer is prepared to be. Could you take some work home? Starting – and leaving – earlier is another possibility, and may be easier to handle if it's officially recognised. When you ask for concessions like these, have solutions ready to offer your employer, so that you can demonstrate that your job will be properly covered.

- Leave work worries behind when you get home and concentrate on your partner and child.

- Beware, if you find yourself thinking that you'll spend more time with your baby once you're less busy at work. That time will never come, unless you take steps to make it happen.

- If your partner is also working full-time she may try to do more than her fair share of childcare in order to compensate. Work out a way of sharing it, instead.

Working part-time

The option chosen by the majority of working mothers, part-time work has the great advantage of being less stressful than full-time work, and allowing women to keep a toe in the working world. But it does carry financial penalties, as part-time jobs are notoriously badly paid and lack many of the financial benefits of full-time posts.

Another solution that some couples consider is for both to have part-time jobs. Laura Wilkinson, writing in *Family Business*, describes how she and her partner planned to do this before their son Morgan was born.

We would enjoy rewarding paid work and share the pleasure and pain that is child rearing. But it has not worked out that way. My husband works full-time and I work part-time. We discovered not only that two part-time jobs don't pay as much as one full-time job, but also that interesting 'career' jobs are usually full time.

Laura is optimistic about the future, but has learned that it takes time to sort out solutions and find the right jobs. She adds:

Despite its voguish portrayal in the press, parenthood is difficult, undervalued work in our society. Finding the balance between work and home, work and parenthood, and making it pay, both emotionally and financially, is very hard.

———————————— **Talk about it** ————————————

- To what extent are you working in order to contribute to the family income? By the time you've paid for childcare you may only just break even.

- If one of you works part-time for personal satisfaction rather than for the money, be sure you are both comfortable with this arrangement. Working creates hassle, and everyone has to be committed to making it all run smoothly.

- Part-time work can involve shifts, or working in evenings or at weekends. Ideally, one minds the baby while the other works, but do schedule in some time when you are both together, and not exhausted. It's so easy for your own relationship to slip down the tubes if you only ever see each other in passing.

Mothers staying at home

Just a dream for many women, as increasingly families need two incomes in order to stay afloat. For some, though, staying at home when the children are small is a very important part of parenthood. Tessa, a keep-fit instructor, had planned to go back to work two days a week after Tom was born, but changed her mind.

I'm not so keen now. I just don't feel like doing it. I'd miss him. My next door neighbour was going to mind him, but I don't want to hand him over. I enjoy looking after him, and I enjoy him. I think that's it now, until he goes to school. We can manage on Simon's money, and Simon prefers it if I look after Tom. So it suits us all.

Think about it

- Make sure both of you are happy to live with a drop in income. Resentments can fester if one partner feels over-burdened, or sees the other as having the soft option.

- Seek out companionship and stimulation outside the home. Once you are no longer working, it's easy to stagnate and come to depend on your partner for all your social stimulation – boring for both of you, and a big responsibility for your partner, too.

Fathers staying at home

Still unusual, but by no means as rare as it was even five years ago, in some families the obvious solution is for the woman to work full-time while the man cares for the children. Relate counsellor Andrew Tyler and his wife did this.

Her job was far better paid than mine, and I knew that if I gave up my job I'd be able to get another one later on, and could probably pick up some part-time work if I wanted to in the meantime. I certainly wasn't the only man around who was caring for children full-time – there were four others in the parent toddler group I went to. Now that both my daughters are at school I can look back and say that it was a wonderful thing to have done. I certainly have a close bond with the children.

_____ **Think about it** _____

• Be aware that taking on responsibility for childcare doesn't suit every man. Cheryl's husband was unemployed when their daughter was born, and looked after her while Cheryl returned to work.

   We continued like this for a couple of years, but he became increasingly fed up with his role – or lack of it. Although he looked after the baby quite successfully, he did assume I would take over whenever I wasn't actually working. Eventually he found a part-time job and our daughter went to a childminder. Having some paid care took the strain off our relationship, so that we were no longer spending all our time passing the child from one to the other.

• Some men could find it hard to lose their job and be dependent on their partner financially. Be clear in your own mind about how much your sense of your own worth is tied up in your job.

• Keep up contact with friends and make sure that you still follow your interests. If you've always played football on Thursday nights or whatever, don't give it up.

• Be careful not to give out the wrong signals. Inevitably you will meet lots of women with their children during the day. You may not be able to form the support relationships you need as easily as a woman could.

Rethinking your working life

Having children can provide an opportunity to start again, either because your old job just doesn't mix with family life, or because it's time for a change. You're also likely to find that the working solution that fits well when you have one child, won't be so good if you go on to have more children. Many women reduce their working hours or even give up work completely for a time once they have more than one child. Flexibility is crucial.

_____ **Talk about it** _____

- Make sure any decisions about a new start are joint decisions. If you're both committed to a long-term goal it is much easier to accept short-term struggles.

- Remember, although life is family-centred now, it won't be forever. In a few short years, life will open up again and many more things will become possible. Plan for the future, even if you can only work towards your goals bit by bit.

- Don't be seduced into thinking that working from home is the answer to all your problems. It does have flexibility, but children still need to be cared for while you work, preferably away from home, so that you can concentrate fully. And deadlines have to be met, regardless of what else is going on in your life.

CHILDCARE

In three out of five families, partners depend on each other, and other family members for childcare. This doesn't work for all, however, since other family members – usually grandparents – may not live nearby or be able to offer childcare.

Finding alternatives can be stressful. There *is* good childcare available and the government promises that there will be more. Finding it, keeping it and paying for it, are obstacles that working parents have to face.

Leaving your child with a childminder or at a nursery can be a gut-wrenching experience. Men can help, if their partner finds it particularly hard, by dropping the baby off.

When Annette returned to work part-time, her baby was three months old.

Left Alex with Nancy for the first time today. Woke up feeling sick at the prospect of parting. Thrust him into her arms and ran back to the car. Cried all the way to work, raced back. He was fine, but I was a wreck.

It does get easier, however. Six months later, Annette wrote:

All is nicely settled now. Alex goes very happily to Nancy and I trust her to look after him well. And I love my time at work really. I look forward to those hours when I can use a different part of my brain, and my personality.

GUILT

Many women put themselves through a lot of anguish over leaving their children. Yet most research shows that, as long as childcare is good, children do not suffer from being separated from their parents. Times have changed, and today's generation of parents take their working and parenting responsibilities very seriously, and make great efforts to devote time to both.

- One study showed that working parents, both women and men, spend more time talking to their children and playing with them than their own parents spent with them.
- Children who see parents working as a team and considering and respecting each others' needs are getting an excellent model for their own relationships in later life.

Perfect parents don't exist. The best you can do is try to meet your children's needs while not ignoring your own. When you make decisions about your work and your family, don't put your own relationship at the bottom of the list of priorities. Give it high importance, value and nurture it, and your family will be stronger and happier for it.

In brief

- Consider taking a new approach to the way you work.

- Your capacity – and desire – to work outside the home may change as the baby grows. Be flexible.

- Make the best arrangements you can, then relax. Children can gain from having working parents, just as much as parents can gain from working.

Chapter 13

MONEY: WORKING OUT A FAIR DEAL

I haven't been earning for nearly a year, and it's starting to cause definite tension. Suddenly there are lots of things we can't talk about – having a holiday, fixing the car, decorating the living room – because they're about money, and about not having enough of it. We'd planned to have another child in about a year or 18 months time, and I'd always said I'd stay home until both children were at school or nursery. But that would be another three or four years on one income – I'm not sure that Phil can hack it. Denise, mother of eight-month Carina

Money. Hot topic for rows at any stage of a relationship, and definitely high on the agenda as a bone of contention for many couples after a baby is born. Why? Because having a baby changes the financial balance in a family.

The traditional set-up where man wins bread while woman stays home is less and less common, as increasingly women with dependent children return to work. Yet stereotyped ideas of how families ought to operate die hard. One survey showed that over half of fathers, and more than 40 per cent of mothers, still think that the man's role is to provide for the family.

The days when men doled out housekeeping money and kept women in ignorance of their salaries have gone. Now it's far more complicated, often with two earners in the household who may have very different financial agendas.

Many people also arrive at parenthood with a handsome collection of financial baggage, left over from having lived independently, or having had other long-standing relationships. They may also be supporting children from previous relationships. No wonder it can be so hard to sort out a way of handling money that leaves everyone satisfied.

THE FINANCIAL EFFECTS OF PARENTHOOD

Parenthood is an expensive business. With an average spend over the first five years of £20,000, not including childcare, it's clear that babies can damage your budget like a bulldozer. If at the same time you lose a proportion of your family income when one of you stops working, you're left with a sum that can look pretty mean to a couple who've been used to spending freely from two incomes.

Some of the most common ways for a baby to impact on your financial lifestyle include the following.

Losing independence/having to accept others' dependence

These two can go hand in hand. A woman used to earning and managing her own money can find it very hard to accept financial dependence on her partner. At the same time, he, having been used to a self-supporting partner, may feel the pressure of having to provide. All of this can be very testing for a couple's relationship.

Had long talk about money, very uncomfortable for both of us. I still get upset by the idea of dependency and having to justify my spending and go to him for cash. But at the same time part of me feels Al should be supporting me – I am look-

ing after the baby full-time, after all. Meanwhile, he's been busy working out exactly what money I have (from interest on my savings, maternity allowance, child benefit); how much I spend and therefore how much he needs to give me to make up the shortfall. Why should I explain to him where every last penny goes – it's demeaning. Moniza

Women in this situation, who have been used to financial independence, may balk at asking their partners for money and instead eke out any savings or money of their own rather than rely on him. A mother of an eight-month baby says:

I'm only managing to work a few hours each week, and what I earn just about covers my standing orders, but doesn't leave me any spending money. Rather than go cap-in-hand to my partner for cash, I'm gradually using money I saved when I was single: I've drained one account and now I'm going to redeem my pension. It doesn't seem to occur to him that I need money and I just cannot bring myself to ask.

Men can also feel resentful at the new demands being made on them. Mark says:

Janetta wants me to transfer £500 a month to her account to keep her afloat. I know she has insurance policies and stuff to pay, but what's the rest going on? Well, the bottom line is I just haven't got it. We're going to have to have a big rethink, or else she's going to have to get back to work – fast.

Loss of control

Along with the loss of financial independence often goes the loss of any right to have a say in financial decisions. This happens if a man decides that as he is now supporting the family, he has a right to spend money as he pleases. This attitude can leave the other feeling powerless and resentful, even when the amounts involved are relatively small.

Matt came home yesterday with three new CDs – when was the last time I bought something for myself on impulse like that? He expected me to be pleased that he got a bargain, but I felt really sick. It's not fair. Lindsay

This loss of bargaining power can extend to much larger issues, such as where a couple live, and can cause great harm in a relationship.

One day Toby came home and said he'd been offered a transfer to a town 200 miles away – and he'd said yes, without even consulting me. I was really upset – I had loads of friends locally, a real support system, and my mum is only ten minutes away. Before Theo was born Toby would have had to talk to me about the implications of a move on my career – I was a teacher. But now his view was that I was no longer tied to a job, he was the breadwinner, it was a better job – and he wanted it. End of discussion. Sabina

Loss of social life

Working couples spend. They eat out, buy takeaways, go to the cinema, spend money on hobbies and holidays. Once a child arrives, not only is there the logistical problem of finding suitable care and getting out of the house at the right time, but it's quite likely that the money for going out just won't be there any more.

A woman who has stopped working to care for a baby can become very dependent on her partner for a while. He represents her link with the outside world, and if money is tight so that she can't get out and mix with other people so readily, and nor can he, and they can't go out together either, both can start to feel trapped and resentful – a recipe for rows.

————————————— **Think about it** —————————————

- Whether you feel too dependent, or too depended-upon, remember that it's not forever. Things will change as your family grows up.

- Imbalances which leave one partner feeling aggrieved or unfairly treated can be very destructive. Tell your partner how you feel and do your best to work together towards a compromise that gives you back some level of control within the relationship.

- Try to understand why you feel bad about the way you are handling money. It may be that you are reminded of your own parents, and if they had rows about money you may fear following the same pattern.

- Change is a necessary part of life and is easier to handle if you accept that it is inevitable and then set about making it positive. It may be tough adapting, but if you can get through this together, you'll emerge stronger on the other side.

WHY PEOPLE ROW ABOUT MONEY

Money is the most common topic for rows, with many arguments focusing on disagreements over how the money is spent. Making it harder is the fact that for many people money, like sex, is still a taboo subject and they don't feel comfortable talking about it.

Row sparkers

These are some of the classic causes of money-based disagreements after a couple have a child.

Spending on the baby She wants delicious new baby equipment and clothing, he reckons secondhand is good enough and is reluctant to spend more.

The woman's return to work She wants to stay home, return part-time, or delay her return. He wants her to return sooner and work longer hours than she would like.

Cost of childcare The tasks of choosing, setting up and paying for childcare, are most frequently shouldered by the woman. She may feel unfairly burdened.

General spending Partners can't agree on priorities; one spends or runs up credit card bills without consulting the other; one spends more than the other; one is secretive or dishonest about money.

Unemployment Losing a job can be a hard blow to withstand and bring feelings of loss, anger and depression.

Talk about it

- Do conversations about money make you feel angry? If so, ask yourself what your underlying feelings are. Anger can be a defence – we lash out in order to avoid feeling the pain, hurt, rejection or anxiety that has been provoked. Start to understand why you respond in the way you do, and you can look for better ways to handle the feelings that money discussions arouse.

- Money conversations often follow a well-worn track, and couples can find themselves going round and round in the same old row, resolving nothing. Next time this starts to happen, ask yourself what it is that you would *really* like to say to your partner. Is there a way to say it that is helpful, and not confrontational? It only takes one person to break the mould for arguments to take on a different pattern, which can help you find workable solutions.

TALKING MONEY

Talking about money takes a particularly high level of trust and openness. People sometimes fear that they will be thought greedy if they want money, or be perceived as caring more about the other person's money than about their feelings.

The best time to start talking about money is before your baby arrives. Lauren and Mick didn't do this, and ended up at Relate when their daughter Holly was six months old because they were fighting non-stop about money. The counsellor tells the story:

They had moved to a large house, with a large mortgage based on both salaries, the year before the baby was born. Although they had not been using contraception in the months before she was conceived, they said they hadn't been ready financially to have a baby. During the pregnancy they'd closed their eyes to money worries: 'We just said, we'll work something out,' said Lauren.

Although they were both delighted with Holly, there just wasn't enough money to make ends meet. Lauren had been very reluctant to return to work because she wanted to stay with Holly. Eventually she'd been forced to go back to work and had taken a nursing job, which involved doing nights two or three times a week.

She had hoped that this way she wouldn't miss out on spending too much time with Holly, and would save the cost of childcare, as Mick would be looking after Holly while she was at work. In fact, both Lauren and Mick had become exhausted, Lauren because she had allowed herself virtually no time to catch up on sleep, and Mick because his nights were disturbed by Holly whenever Lauren was working. Tired beyond belief and unable to see a way out of their problems, they were arguing constantly.

Over several months, counselling helped them unravel their feelings, stop blaming each other, and start looking for a better solution. Eventually, they took the radical step of selling their house and moving to a smaller one, with a lower mortgage. Once this had reduced their outgoings to more manageable levels, Lauren changed to working two days a week, while Holly went to a nursery. As everyone became less tired, and less pressurised, the rows dwindled.

If Lauren and Mick had worked out their finances earlier on, they might not have bought such an expensive house, or might have delayed starting a family for a year or two. Potential problems are far easier to resolve if you anticipate them. Use shared thinking and planning to tackle problems before they arise.

Talk about it

- Do a comparative budget: take your combined incomes now and list your expenses. Then work out what you expect your income/expenditure to be after the baby is born.

- Make a baby budget, and agree on how much you will earmark to spend on things for the baby.

- Do either of you have any savings which could be used now, and do you agree on how this money will be used?

- Ask friends and relatives with children for tips on how they manage their money.

- Be honest about any debts you have. It will be harder to pay off credit card bills once you have a child, and you may need to work out a plan for clearing debt gradually.

- Talk now about how it would feel to be financially dependent on your partner, or how it would feel to be responsible for supporting the whole family.

- Ask yourselves questions. Don't make assumptions about the answers, and try to listen carefully to each other.
  - Who will pay for what?
  - Who will decide how we spend our money?
  - If one partner's income is reducing, how will she/he meet personal expenses?
  - How will we organise our money?

FINDING NEW WAYS OF MANAGING MONEY

Almost inevitably, a change in income and spending patterns will mean that you have to find a new way of managing money. There are several possibilities.

Main breadwinner One partner (usually the man) manages the money, and gives the other an allowance. A traditional approach, this works better if both have a say in how money is spent, even if the money manager writes the cheques. It demands shared ideas and agreement on spending to work well.

Everything pooled In this scenario, all the income goes into a joint account, which both partners can draw on. Twenty-five per cent of couples manage their finances this way. It works well if both individuals have similar attitudes to spending, and if neither is reckless with money.

Partial pooling The couple run a joint account for shared expenses to which both contribute an agreed amount if they can. Each also has an independent account for personal expenses. This can become difficult if one stops working and therefore cannot 'feed' either the joint account or their own account. In this case, the couple need to agree on a sum that the earner will transfer to the non-earner for personal expenses, and another sum that the earner will transfer to the joint account on which both can draw for agreed expenses.

STEPFAMILIES

The whole question of money can be particularly difficult within a stepfamily. Say, for instance, a couple where one partner already has children, have a child together. It's easy for resentment to start over the money spent on the previous family. Sometimes, a parent who is parted from his or her children may use money to try to compensate for absence, or for the arrival of a new baby. Couples in these types of situation need extra sensitivity and insight to sort things out.

MONEY MATTERS

Money is a very powerful tool. When well handled it can represent a couple's shared commitment and trust in each other, as well as demonstrating their acceptance of a new balance within their relationship now that they have a family. But it can also represent so much more, both to the partner who has money, and the one who does not. Money can bring status, power, freedom, which parenthood removes. Be sure you have thought about it carefully.

In brief

- There's nothing like money problems to trigger off huge rows.
- A drop in income can seriously bruise your spending plans. Think ahead, before you start to feel the pinch.
- Earning money gives women an independence that is sometimes sorely missed.

PART FOUR

THRIVING AS A COUPLE

Chapter 14
TIME FOR YOURSELVES

When our two-year-old spent her first night with her grand-parents, we drove 20 miles away and stayed the night at a country hotel. We had a huge dinner, woke up late next morning and made love before getting up, sat around for ages over breakfast and the papers. Then we went for a long, long walk. It was so good to be able to talk if we wanted or to be able to walk in silence, just enjoying being together. Yes, we did miss Jessie, and by the time we went to pick her up I was longing to see her. But it was great to have that time just for us – I think we need to do it more often.
Bryony

It is very easy to get out of the habit of spending time together, once you have a family, but it is very important to try and make that time, and make it regularly. Neglect your relationship and you run the risk of resurfacing years later different people from the ones you were before – and poles apart.

In among the chaos of those first weeks, it can be impossible to get any 'real' time with your partner that doesn't revolve around the baby. It's important to be aware of this, so that not having time for each other doesn't become a habit. A Relate counsellor says:

People think that their coupledom will stay alive because they are committed to each other. Parents tend to divert towards the children all the time, instead of focusing on their own relationship. They think that that will somehow take care of itself, but often it won't. You, as a couple, have to make very particular efforts to protect it. Ask yourselves, How can we make the space to keep ourselves going as a couple?

Sometimes the only way to grab a bit of uninterrupted time is to make up your minds that you're going to have it. Donna described one evening, when her baby, Rory, was about six months old:

Couldn't get Rory to go down. He cried for an hour before dropping off. Raced downstairs to cook, but just as we were about to eat, there it was again over the baby alarm. I was so tired, I said, 'I can't go up again.' In desperation, we turned the baby alarm off. Turned it on again after five minutes, 'Waaaaah,' so gave it another five minutes – silence. And then he slept through. Perhaps we should learn to harden our hearts, just a little.

_____ **Try this** _____

Linda Connell of PIPPIN uses this technique to prepare couples for life with their baby. PIPPIN courses (see page 218) focus on providing support for couples during the natural and often challenging changes that occur for all men and women when a child is born.

Before the birth I ask couples to think of the things that each of them love doing together. Then we talk about how it will be once the baby comes, and how it might not be so easy to do these things, at least for a while and sometimes for the long term. I ask them, if you only had five minutes in a day to do something as a couple, what would it be? Then they can start

*enlarging it – what about ten minutes, or half an hour.
Suppose the baby was being looked after by someone you
trusted, what would you do in a whole evening together?*

*People sometimes think that because they can't go out to
the cinema together when their baby is tiny, or whatever it
was they particularly used to enjoy, that they are no longer
being a couple. Actually, though, you can be a couple in one
minute, five minutes or whatever time you have during the
day. The important thing is to snatch those moments, and
use them to talk, laugh, touch, and generally catch up with
each other.*

TIME TOGETHER

From relishing fragments here and there when your baby
is tiny, you can gradually move on to getting more time to
yourselves and regain closeness. Don't ignore your need for
time together, or make excuses for not organising it. Yes, it
does take effort to set up, and you may also be pulled by
the desire not to be parted from your child. But children
often respond well to having a fresh person looking after
them and, by separating from them for short periods,
and leaving them with people you trust, you are setting up
patterns that can stand you in good stead right through
their childhood.

Pippa and Martin are the parents of four girls, the
youngest of whom is now 12.

*We've always had one night out together since they were tiny,
and often it's been the only chance we've had for a conversation all week. With four small children in the house, there
was always someone crying or wanting attention. Every
Friday my next door neighbour used to come in at 7.30pm,
and we'd go off down to the pub. It was only five minutes*

away, but it felt like going into a different world, full of adults. These days it's still just as hard to have a conversation at home, especially since the older girls go to bed later than we do. So we still go down to the pub on Friday nights, and leave the older girls in charge. Pippa

Another mother has a regular lunchtime slot booked for her baby with a childminder so that once a week she can have lunch with her husband.

————————— **Think about it** —————————

- Spending time together can mean doing something quite low-key, like going for a walk, or out for a drink. Just an hour is enough, if that's all you can manage.

- Don't automatically refuse invitations out, just because making arrangements is a bit of a hassle. You could get stuck in the habit of saying no after things have become easier.

- In the very early days it can be easy to take the baby along with you, but as soon as he or she stops being portable, start going out on your own.

- Go out regularly and make it part of your routine.

- Try to find time to talk when you're out – if you see a film, have a drink afterwards.

- By all means talk about the children – it would be unusual if you didn't – but try to look beyond them as well, and keep a foothold in the wider world.

YOUR RELATIONSHIP IS FIRST PRIORITY

Counsellors often see the results when people have neglected their relationships by always putting their children first. A Relate counsellor says:

Once you have a baby you get on to this treadmill of babies/children and by the time you wake up 10 or 15 years later the problems are huge and you've just been sitting on them. People are so responsible about their parenting, but they completely discount themselves and their relationship. They feel they can't say, Go away children, we're going to do such and such. All these years they've just assumed their relationship will be OK, and then it falls apart. When they come for counselling, it's part of my role to 'give permission' for them to spend time together alone, but it meets with huge resistance.

Beth and Clive gave up going out together when their children were small because it was simply too much hassle.

Things did get bad, though, when Clive's career took off and we were hardly spending any time together. Our relationship started to deteriorate – we were constantly bickering and retreating into separate lives. We lost sight of the things we love about each other, and saw only annoying habits, perceived lack of support and so on. These days we aim to go out together once a week, but it's usually more like once a fortnight. It's always worth making the effort and it gives you a chance to tackle any problems as you go along, before they get too big. We also do sports activities on our own, which helps to get things in perspective if we are feeling wound up. I also see several close women friends regularly, and once or twice a year escape on my own for a 'girls' weekend' while Clive looks after the children.

_____ **Try this** _____

- Time together doesn't have to happen outside the home. You can squeeze stray moments into most days.

- Keep up with the rituals you used to have. Have a drink together in the early evening, or cuddle up together on the sofa to watch TV.

- Turn the TV off at the end of the programme.

- Institute a regular bedtime for children from babyhood – and stick to it. This can be tough, but your health visitor or GP can advise you on techniques to achieve it, and the pay-off is enormous. If you can be sure of a few undisturbed hours during the evening you'll be doing yourselves a lot of favours.

- Now and then, go to bed early, together.

- A couple of minutes' chat about your days, a caress when you pass each other or a quick kiss, all of these make you both feel loved and valued even in the maelstrom of family demands.

GETTING SUPPORT FROM OTHER PEOPLE

No couple is an island. If you can share the load beyond the two of you, even a bit, it can make all the difference to the amount of stress you feel, and free you up to enjoy each others' company.

Babysitters

Every family needs to find reliable babysitters, whom they like and trust. A Relate counsellor says:

It's surprising how much some people resist the idea of babysitters. I've heard every excuse in the book as to why people can't get out together. Often, it's a sign that there's something amiss within their relationship, which they'd prefer not to confront. If a parent wants to hide something, they will often use the child as an excuse for not spending time with their partners.

Even if that's not the case, many people make heavy weather of the babysitter question. Young children can put on a lot of emotional pressure to stop their parents going out. Deirdre's son Adam tried this tactic:

When he was small John and I didn't go out until we knew he was asleep, usually by 7.30pm. I made sure that he'd met the babysitter and liked her, so he wouldn't have been totally astonished if he'd woken up, but I didn't tell him when she was coming. When he got older I decided that honesty was the best policy, so I used to tell him on the day, that we were going out that evening. To start with, he created merry hell, crying and wailing. Louise, our babysitter, was great – she told us to go, and I rang home after 15 minutes. She'd distracted him and he'd stopped crying almost immediately. Soon, he began to look forward to her coming because he knew she gave him such a fun time, and now he asks us when we're next going out! I would advise anyone to persevere. I still love going out with my husband – it feels like such a treat and setting it up has been well worth a little anguish. And I believe Adam has benefited as much as we have.

Many teenage girls, and some boys, enjoy babysitting and find it a useful way to earn a bit of pocket money. Choose someone who is 16 or older and get reliable references. Leave the babysitter with a telephone number so they can contact you and an emergency number of a nearby neighbour or friend. Make sure they have met your child once or twice before babysitting for the first time. Then go out and enjoy yourselves.

_____ **Try this** _____

- Join a babysitting circle, or set one up. Parents babysit for each other and use a point or token system for payment. Advantages are that no money is involved, and other parents are experienced at dealing with children and may know your child well. A disadvantage is that you have to do some babysitting yourself in order to clock up credit, which can eat into your free time.

- Ask grandparents or other relatives to help out. Organise an occasional night or weekend if they are willing.

- When children are a little older, 'swap' with friends who have children the same age to give each other a break during the day, or overnight.

_____

TIME FOR YOURSELF

As well as a chance to be together as a couple, parents also need time to themselves as individuals. Just to go for a walk without a child in tow can be a marvellous experience for a parent who is used to doing everything at a child's pace.

Geraldine's husband Richard takes over with baby Louis on Saturday morning while she goes out for a couple of hours.

First Saturday 'off' – wow! Walked fast and free, strode along, swinging my bag. Even going to the greengrocer and mulling over the avocados was a real liberation.

Think about it

- Plan your 'time off' from the baby – put it on the calendar or in your diary if it helps to make sure it really happens.

- Aim for at least half an hour to yourself every day, and don't spend it doing chores. Use the time to relax in the bath, read the paper, phone a friend. You'll feel better for it.

- Ask yourselves, what do I enjoy? What do I miss? Then make efforts to let each other do these things. Don't expect this to happen immediately. Tiredness, plus lack of money and time are all constraints. Katy remembers:

  To start with I just felt too shattered to go out, although I did miss the friends I had at the tennis club. That first summer I only played twice, but by the second summer I was feeling much more like it, so Damian used to take the baby out every Saturday afternoon while I got a game in. I really appreciated that.

- Make sure that both of you get similar amounts of free time.

- Beware of over-filling your lives: it's bad for your health and your relationship, and the effects creep up, almost unnoticed. Michel, father of 5-year-old Joseph and 2-year-old Angelique, reflects:

  Before the children I used to do a lot of sport – badminton twice a week, squash. But now, with both of us working full-time and the children so young, I haven't played since Angelique was born. This last six months Pascal and I have both been ill and tired. We desperately need the chance to relax more and catch up with some of the things we used to enjoy.

TIME WITH FRIENDS

Friends can make up an important part of your support system, but even long-established friendships can change once you have a child. Friends who do not have children may feel that they are losing you, or find it hard to accept and understand the new demands that are being made on you. Dee had worked in a publishing company before she left to have Jack. One of her best friends at work was Jo, who was still working.

She used to ring me up at 6.30pm, just before she left work, for a catch-up. It was the worst possible time for me as Jack was usually gruesome in the early evening. One night she rang and I said, 'I just can't talk now,' and Jo said, 'Oh, I suppose he's crying again, is he?' and put the phone down. She did apologise later, but the damage was done.

GOING ON HOLIDAY

Before babies, holidays for most couples are a time of glorious relaxation – a chance to step off the treadmill of everyday working life and get reacquainted. Sex often improves too, with the freedom to fall into bed at any time of day. Children change all that. Kate Figes sums it up in *Life After Birth*.

Holidays with small children are often not very peaceful for the grown-ups. They find themselves guiltily looking forward to going back to work for a rest.

It's true, holidays with children are different from holidays without, and for some couples this can be a big problem. Sam and Polly came to Relate when their son Jay was one year old. The counsellor remembers:

At first all their problems seemed to be about holidays. Sam especially liked active adventure holidays, and before Jay arrived he and Polly had been skiing, rock climbing and deep-sea diving together. Now, he said, he still wanted to do those things, but Polly just wanted to laze around with Jay.

In counselling, it emerged that Sam's father had died the previous year, which had really shaken him up. He had a feeling that he must cram everything he wanted to do into his life, and the sooner the better. He'd come face to face with his own mortality and wanted to do his own thing now, because life doesn't last forever. Becoming a parent, although he'd gone into it willingly, didn't fit with those feelings.

The couple's differences over holidays acted as a focus for a lot of surrounding dissatisfactions. They had to work at many other areas of their relationship before things improved. When it came to holidays, they agreed that Sam would be 'allowed' to take an active holiday once a year by himself, and that Polly would accept his need to do that. Fortunately he had a well-paid job, so they were able to do this and have a holiday together as a family as well.

Think about it

- Family holidays can be stressful. Consider having a couple of short breaks rather than one long one, and spreading them out over the year.

- Try holidays that provide a crèche service or have supervised children's activities so that you can get a break.

- Consider going on holiday with another family and sharing some of the childcare.

DO IT NOW

There are masses of ways you can find little bits of time to spend together and by yourselves. Some may take more effort than others, but all are worthwhile. Little bits add up and can become bigger bits as children get older. Counsellor Lucy Selleck tells couples:

Your relationship must come over and above the children, because if it does and you are happy together, then your children will reap the benefits. It certainly isn't selfish, unless you take it to extremes. If you are looking after your relationship, you are without a doubt looking after your children. It is in their prime interest that you remain a loving, committed couple for them. You can only do that if your relationship is in prime place, and that means spending time on it, taking care of it, thinking about it and nurturing it.

In brief

- Don't give up on ever having time for each other. Start with a few minutes here and there, then build.

- Use family, friends and babysitters to give you the odd hour of freedom.

- Time spent staying in touch with each other now will pay dividends when children are older.

- As well as couple-time, schedule in some me-time whenever you can.

Chapter 15

IS THERE SEX AFTER CHILDBIRTH?

I knew Ike was counting the days until my postnatal examination. That morning he said, 'Tonight's the night,' as he left. But I wasn't feeling like it. Yes, my body might have healed, physically there was no reason for me not to have sex, but I was tired out – all I wanted to do in bed was sleep, sleep, sleep. Darina

Talk to any group of mothers with babies about how their relationship has changed, and the first thing they're likely to say is, 'No sex!' Lisa, mother of 18-month-old Charlie, remarks ruefully:

People ask me when I'm going to have another baby, and I say it'll have to be an immaculate conception.

SEX IN THE EARLY DAYS

In the early days after a baby's birth, it's not surprising that sex is nowhere on the agenda. Quite apart from disturbed nights and tiredness, a woman may have sore breasts, stitches and tender genitals to cope with, or she may be recovering from a Caesarean section. The last thing she feels like is passionate sex. The postnatal examination, six weeks after the birth, gives the green light to go ahead with sex provided everything is well physically. Frankly, though, the majority of couples take many months to get back to any semblance of a regular sex life and the process is gradual.

What's changed?

These are just some of the many reasons why sex changes after the birth of a baby.

- Lose habit of having sex, especially if it was uncomfortable during pregnancy.
- Tired and stressed. Afraid of waking baby.
- Loss of desire.
- Prolonged or traumatic birth can put you off sex afterwards.
- Woman may get such deep satisfaction from her baby, that she has less need for physical intimacy with her partner.
- Woman feels less physically desirable than before.
- Postnatal depression – see page 178.
- Avoiding any physical intimacy in case your partner takes it as a sign of wanting sex.
- Seeing your partner in a new light, as 'mother' or 'father', can alter your view of them sexually as well.
- If your sex life was previously unsatisfactory, the baby can provide an excuse for having sex less often, or not at all.

That's quite a list, and it goes a long way to explaining why, for many new parents, sex is but a distant dream. Verena, mother of 16-week-old Josh, writes:

Sex? What's that? Sam says he feels tired to the point of losing touch with himself. And I'm just constantly aching behind the eyes, and by bedtime am worn out. We need to try and sort out other times when we could make love although, to be honest, sex is still rather painful for me, which puts me off a bit. And it's so easy just to focus on the baby all the time, and forget about our relationship.

For some couples, the joy aroused by their child does lead to an easier return to loving intimacy. Joe, father of a ten-week-old, says:

Maeve and I have probably had more slow, tender sex in this wonderful postnatal high, while Mollie is asleep in her cot, than we had had for months. But I suspect it won't last – already it's getting harder to find a time when she's sleeping and we aren't too tired.

PHYSICAL PROBLEMS

Often there are physical reasons why sex is uncomfortable, or even downright painful, for a great many women in the weeks after giving birth. Episiotomy, stitches, bruising from a forceps delivery, all these take time to heal. If things still aren't right at your six-week check, tell the doctor and ask for further investigations if necessary.

As well as discomfort arising from the birth itself, women also have to contend with many changes in their body. One mother of a six-week-old says gloomily:

My vagina's about the same size as the local swimming pool now.

Over the next few months many of the changes do become less obvious or disappear completely. But for most women, the body they have after giving birth is not the body they had before. This can be sad and can make a woman feel unattractive. It's vital that men are understanding and kind to their partners about these changes that are just one of the many differences that becoming parents will make to you. Many women come to be proud of their new bodies:

Well, it shows I've done it. I've got a woman's body now, not a girl's.

Sometimes, however, changes brought about by pregnancy and birth can be seriously distressing, as in Natascha's case.

I'd always felt lucky as far as my body was concerned: there were no ugly or embarrassing bits. I was at ease with my clothes off and enjoyed uninhibited sex, almost till the day my first child was born.

About eight months into my first pregnancy, however, I developed dark purple lightning streaks fanning out from my belly button. I carried on putting the moisturiser on daily and tried not to worry about the obscene map spreading across my tummy. My son was born by emergency Caesarean. Six months later my purple-lined abdomen had turned into a brownish crater of heavy wrinkles that I could literally pile up above either hip. My skin had been stretched beyond its natural elasticity and was now simply a flaccid sac, like a wrinkly old balloon left lying after a party. Where was my much loved, much enjoyed beautiful body? Gone. Gone forever it seemed, and I choked back tears each time I looked in the mirror.

To love and enjoy your body seems to me the ideal way of being and I had had that pleasure – and my husband with me. But from the day my son was born nobody was allowed to see my body, least of all my husband. Sex, if it happened at all, was a horrible travesty of what we had had before, something fumbled in the dark, something two strangers might have done, but not two loving and exuberant lovers. Gradually I spoke about my feelings, told my husband how upset I was, how I hated myself, how my self-image was totally destroyed and how unsexy I felt. He said it didn't matter. But it did.

Natascha's disfigurement blighted her sex life for several years, until after the birth of her second son. Doctors were unsympathetic, treating her as if she was vain and superficial for even mentioning it. Her case was not considered important, therefore plastic surgery was not on offer under the NHS.

Four years after having first set eyes on my changed shape I finally cried about it. Grieved for the body I had lost that would never come back, no matter what. Never, not once, in all those years did my husband make me feel ugly, nor act as if he no longer wanted me. I cannot say how grateful I am to him for that. Now another year has gone by and I am finally able to play freely with my husband again – at least by candlelight – and my children can laugh about my wrinkly tummy and it is OK.

Natascha's case was rare, but her feelings about her altered body will be familiar to many women whose bodies have changed less radically. Becoming a mother heralds a shift in sexuality, which can have profound effects on a couple's sexual relationship, and it can take great love and understanding to come through it together.

'YOU NEVER FEEL LIKE IT ANY MORE'

A very, very common problem. As many as 80 per cent of new mothers, and a lot of new fathers, report that sexual desire plummets in the months following the birth of a baby. Not having sex, especially if it was an important part of your lives before, can be very distressing.

Partners need to treat each other with great understanding and affection in order to avoid feeling rejected. Try to keep the physical side of your relationship going, even if you don't actually have intercourse. If day-to-day intimacy slides too much, it is much harder to get back into it again when you start to feel more interested.

Dominique and Jim stopped having sex in the early days of her pregnancy. It was Jim who went off it – Dominique would have liked to have sex. This was just the beginning of many problems, rooted in the fact that Jim did not really want to be having a baby. As Dominique retreated into herself and became more and more centred on herself and her unborn child, he felt more and more excluded. Things didn't improve after the baby was born and, although this couple did have counselling, eventually they separated. Their counsellor explains:

Pregnancy can be quite isolating for men, and women need to be aware of that. That's where sex comes in. Most people still do have sex during pregnancy, but some feel that they shouldn't, or they don't want to. It is so important to keep intimacy going though, even if you don't have penetrative sex. There are 101 other things you can do that are intimate, loving and may be extremely satisfying. If you give up on sex altogether there's a risk of the relationship dying, as this one did.

_____ **Try this** _____

- Give each other a massage, without expecting it to lead to full sex.

- If you both want to, use gentle caresses or oral sex to bring each other to orgasm, rather than trying penetration.

- Make opportunities for physical closeness. Put the baby down and touch each other. Hold hands, sit close together, exchange a caress or kiss when you pass. All these things make it easier for the sexual relationship to return.

- Don't retreat to opposite sides of the bed. Make a habit of having a cuddle and kiss every night. Be clear that this isn't necessarily a prelude to sex.

- Tackle exhaustion. Research shows that many people are so shattered after a long day at work or home that they simply have no energy left for sex.

- Reduce your commitments in any way you can, and go to bed earlier – much earlier – on a regular basis.

- Talk about how you are feeling. Try not to accuse, judge or reject.

- Stay in touch with things that are going on in each others' lives. If there is no real contact between you away from the bedroom, there isn't likely to be much happening once you get to bed, either.

- Remember that the situation is probably only temporary, and don't withdraw emotionally if you feel rejected physically.

THREE IN A BED

Robin arrives beside his parents' bed, early in the morning. 'Come on then,' she whispered. 'Don't wake Daddy.' They watched Max's dark bearded face break into a yawn, a bearded seadog or a seagod about to rally his crew. He was waking up. Robin wriggled under the bedclothes to hide. . . .

Max's eyes flickered awake and he smiled at Dorrie.

'Mmmm,' he said. 'Come here.' He reached over and grabbed her, buried his face in her neck, and then as he reached downwards his hands encountered his son.

'No! No!' screeched Robin, laughing hectically. 'Get away, Daddy!'

This snippet from Helen Simpson's book, *Hey Yeah Right, Get a Life* will strike a resounding chord with many parents. Most small children like nothing better than to clamber into the lovely warmth of mummy and daddy's bed early in the morning, and a fair few like to spend the whole night there. It's all very cosy and intimate, but the constant presence of a third small party can wreak havoc with your sex life. Counsellor Lucy Selleck says:

Having a baby, and later on a toddler, frequently in the bed is one of the most difficult things you can do to your relationship, and is a common cause of sexual problems. By putting a child in the bed, you are creating a barricade, and are making a powerful statement to your partner – You come second now. Even if you can manage to make love quietly while the child sleeps next to you, their presence can be very inhibiting.

Breastfeeding that continues for months after the child is otherwise weaned sometimes has the same effect on a couple's relationship. Lucy Selleck continues:

The sight of their partner breastfeeding, once the child no longer needs the nourishment of her milk, can be quite off-putting for some men. If prolonged breastfeeding becomes a problem, women need to ask themselves who they are doing it for – for the child or for themselves? And where do their partner's needs fit into the equation?

Tara and Jed went to Relate because there were many problems in their relationship. In counselling, it emerged that their three-year-old daughter had been sharing their bed since birth. They had no sex life at all – it had stopped completely. The real problem was that Jed hadn't felt able to admit just how much he wanted the child out of their bed because he felt very guilty about it. Once or twice they had tried to persuade the child to sleep in her own bed, but she kept coming back and they'd given up.

Tara was horrified when she realised how Jed felt. Having Leanna in bed with them had become a habit and Tara had never fully thought through the consequences – or had chosen not to. The couple decided to take a firmer stand with the child and, after a few disrupted nights, broke the pattern. Even then it was some time before their sex life resumed satisfactorily – a distance had grown between them and it took a while to re-establish affection and trust.

It's not just in bed that children impinge on your space and time. They are there during the day and often into the evening and, much as you might enjoy having them around, they make spontaneous lovemaking impossible. Inventive parents, who want to keep their sex life going, have to use guile and cunning to get a bit of uninterrupted time. Roger's two children are five and eight.

The video shop is our salvation. We make love downstairs when they're watching TV upstairs, or downstairs when they're in bed. Sometimes I get the odd day at home to do paperwork, and Em has occasional weekdays off if she's working Saturdays, so if we're both home together we can give coffee breaks a whole new meaning.

Opportunities are greater for Roger and Em because their children are at school. Other problems that started after a birth can also be resolved with the passing of time, although it can take several years. Maya says:

After our first child was born we got back to sex fairly quickly – it wasn't so frequent because we were both so tired, but after about a year or 18 months it was OK. After our second child, however, I went right off it – nothing Steve did could get me aroused. It was as if my body had closed down. Looking back on it, I think I probably had postnatal depression coupled with exhaustion. It was two years before I started to get some sensation back, and really it's taken another couple of years after that to get back to the kind of sex life we had before the children were born.

Yes, it has caused a lot of rows and upset. Initially Steve felt very rejected and eventually he withdrew. For a long time there was no physical contact between us whatsoever. I'd become very uptight about it and was afraid of him touching me in case I didn't get turned on and ended up rejecting him again. Eventually we did manage to talk about it and, once he understood that it was a physical thing with me and not to do with him personally, things started to improve. He was very patient and we used to spend a lot of time in bed just holding each other, softly caressing, with no pressure to have sex. That made both of us feel more loved and, as I began to relax, the desire gradually came back. If Steve hadn't been so patient and understanding, I really think we might have split up over it.

IS SEX THE REAL PROBLEM?

It is very common for a lack of sexual desire to spring from a basic dissatisfaction with other aspects of a relationship. Will and Maisie went to Relate when their son was six because their sex life had become so bad that Maisie was refusing even to share a bed with Will.

She wanted sex less and less after Nathaniel was born, whereas I wanted it as much as ever. She said I behaved like I just had to give her a quick cuddle and then we could move straight on to sex. But I always felt I had to rush it, before she had a chance to pull away. As things got worse and worse we stopped talking, and I had a couple of flings. When we eventually saw a counsellor, Maisie said she'd been angry with me for years because I'd started staying out late, drinking too much and not doing enough to help her with Nathaniel.*

The underlying anger in this couple's relationship had festered into a deep resentment over the years. Unable to reconcile their differences, they eventually divorced.

—————————— **Think about it** ——————————

There is a range of common problems that can affect sex:

- drifting apart
- arguing a lot
- feeling neglected or unloved
- worries over work or money
- affairs

If any of these are relevant to your relationship, look for ways to tackle the root problem. You may well find that if you can get closer again, or stop arguing so much, your sex life will improve of its own accord.

TALKING ABOUT SEX

Sex, more than any other topic, can be virtually impossible to talk about. Revealing feelings to do with sex can make you vulnerable and afraid, and your partner feel inadequate or attacked. There are techniques you can use to make it a lot easier to talk about sex.

_____ **Try this** _____

- Be very aware of your partner's feelings. Don't accuse – 'You never spend long enough on foreplay.' Try making gentle suggestions – 'It feels so nice when you stroke me all over. I'd like you to do it for longer next time.'

- Don't feel you can only talk about sex when you're actually in bed. It can be easier to talk about it away from the scene of the action.

- Get used to talking about sex in a more general way by watching TV programmes about it together or cutting out magazine articles to show your partner.

- Read the Relate guide *Sex in Loving Relationships* for more ideas.

LOOKING TO THE FUTURE

When you are living together in a longterm committed relationship it's important to maintain a sex life that is good for you both. Problems over sex once children are born can be particularly difficult to sort out. Take your time and be patient with each other.

Persevere, but don't put a lot of pressure on each other. Be loving and considerate, and don't stop showing each other how much you care, even if your sex life isn't perfect at the moment. Sex, like every other aspect of life, goes through many changes during the course of a long relationship. Just because things aren't right at one point, doesn't mean they'll never be right again. Give it time and stay relaxed. If things don't start to improve after a while, consider seeking advice from a Relate sex therapist – their job is to help.

_____ **In brief** _____

- Re-establishing a good sex life is a slow process.

- Show physical affection with cuddles and caresses, even if you don't feel like making love.

- A child in the bed is a very effective chastity belt – beware.

Chapter 16

DISAGREEMENTS AND ROWS

Nowadays we argue about little things – who's the most tired, who's worked harder, who deserves a break. Sometimes we argue about the way we look after the children. But we get it over with quickly and accept that we're both tired and need to let off steam. Often we know that the argument is caused by a bad day, so we don't take it to heart. It is important to be sure of one another and understand each other's reactions, otherwise the stress of having kids would certainly drive you apart. Gaynor

Most couples argue, but some argue much more than others. A survey carried out by Relate and Candis found that people with children under ten were the most likely to have frequent rows, and parents in the 18–34 age group with children under four were the most argumentative of all.

Once a couple have children, things that didn't seem so important before can start to cause ructions. The touchiest area is money, but couples also fight about work, children, housework, sex and balancing work and home, all topics close to the hearts of parents who are struggling to find enough time for all the important concerns in their lives.

Rows are a fact of life for most people. In the survey, only one couple in five said they hardly ever argued, while more than one-third fight at least once a week.

Most people find rows unpleasant and upsetting and, while some arguments are trivial and soon forgotten, others reverberate for much longer and can do lasting damage. This chapter looks at the underlying reasons for rows, identifies destructive patterns and suggests ways of handling disagreements better so that they don't cause lasting bad feeling.

WHY ARGUE?

A straightforward row – she forgot to pick up the dry cleaning; he walked across the carpet in muddy boots – soon blows over. It's when arguments spring out of an underlying grievance that resolving differences can become more difficult. When you have a child, emotions change and some couples find they are having more rows, because their feelings have altered.

Row caused by	Hidden issues
Money: how you spend it, how much you have	Insecurity, trust. Fear of dependency
Work: spending too much time at work, promotion, redundancy, returning to work after having children	Partner feels neglected. Jealousy, rivalry. Feeling pulled in different directions.
Time: coming home late, not enough spent together, not enough spent with children	Insecurity, feeling unwanted, fear of growing apart
Sex: not having it frequently enough, finding it less exciting than before	Feeling unloved and unattractive. Fear of partner's infidelity. Fear of being swamped by parenthood and losing touch with own sexuality
Housework: not sharing it fairly	Feeling taken for granted, used, unloved
Children: disagreements about handling; woman acts the expert, man feels inadequate	Feeling criticised, undervalued, unneeded

Sandy and Matt were a classic case where the apparent reason for their constant arguments masked a deeper source of dissatisfaction. Their counsellor remembers:

They came to Relate because they were always fighting about the children. He thought she was totally useless because she didn't discipline them enough. When he came home from work the children were still up and Sandy seemed incapable of getting them to bed – that sort of thing. And this used to cause dreadful rows, in front of the children.

When Sandy and Matt looked more deeply at their pattern of disagreement, it became clear that there was more to their rows than the bedtime question.

Gradually it emerged that Sandy felt totally unsupported by Matt. She had a passive personality and didn't feel at ease with her own authority, either over the children or within the relationship. She had come to feel that she didn't have any rights, and underneath she was very angry about this. Keeping the children up, or doing other things she knew Matt would disapprove of, was her way of saying, 'Look here, I matter too – look at me as a person, don't write me off as an inadequate mother.' She felt abandoned by him, and one simple reason why she didn't get the children to bed on time was because she liked their company – Matt always worked late.

DESTRUCTIVE WAYS OF ARGUING

When it comes to predicting the outcome on your relationship, the *way* you fight is far more revealing than how often you fight. American psychologist John Gottman has been able to predict which couples will divorce, just by listening to them argue for a few minutes. It's not the simple fact that they have arguments that rings alarm bells – some couples have numerous rows, every day, yet stay together happily for years. No, it's how they conduct those arguments that points the finger towards those relationships that are headed for the icebergs.

John Gottman, in his book *The Seven Principles for Making Marriage Work*, identifies four destructive patterns of arguing. Couples who use these tactics when they fight not only stand a poor chance of resolving their differences in any constructive way, but could find that their whole relationship is on the skids unless they make some fundamental changes in the way they approach disagreements.

Being defensive

It's very easy to succumb to the temptation to defend yourself, if you feel attacked by your partner during a row. But being on the defensive seldom makes your partner see your side of the story. Instead, he or she is likely to feel attacked and blamed, because defensiveness carries an implication that the problem lies with the other person. For instance:

Sally*: It would help a lot if you did more around the house. Couldn't you do a bit of vacuuming at the weekend?*

Nick*: I can't see why I should – you've got nothing else to do all day except housework.*

Sally: (defensive) *That's ridiculous! I have a million things to do with the baby, never mind all the cooking and washing. You haven't got a clue just how busy I am all day.*

Nick: *Well, so what. I'm busy too, and I'm too tired at weekends to start messing about with housework.*

When Sally went on the defensive, in an attempt to make Nick see how unreasonable his accusation was, his response was not, 'Poor darling, I hadn't realised how busy you were.' Instead, her defensiveness put him on the defensive too –

the row is starting to escalate and will probably end in stalemate.

Criticising

Few couples never find anything to complain about in their partner's behaviour, but while a complaint focuses on a specific incident, a criticism embellishes this with some well-chosen words about the individual and his or her behaviour in general.

Sally: (complaint) *I'm really angry that you went to bed last night without sterilising the bottles.*
Nick: *Sorry. Forgot.*
Sally: (criticism) *Well that's just typical, isn't it. You always conveniently forget when you don't want to do so something, then I get lumbered. You never give a damn about my feelings.*
Nick: *Look, I just forgot, OK?* (walks out, slamming door)

The complaint that turns into a criticism deflects attention away from the real issue – the bottles that weren't sterilised – and turns the whole argument into a more general attack on Nick and his lack of caring. Feeling attacked and threatened, he refuses to climb down and walks out, leaving bad feelings on both sides – and the bottles still unsterilised.

Criticism is very common in close relationships. Most of us succumb to a bit of character-assassination about our partners now and again, with no great harm done. However, when criticism becomes a habit, it can very easily slide into something far worse – contempt.

Showing contempt

Sarcasm, belligerence, mockery and sneering feature on the script of many arguments. Tactics like these are intended to wound and humiliate the other and, if used frequently, erode affection and respect. Contempt is often born out of prolonged disenchantment with your partner, a feeling which is more likely to develop if you have a pattern of never sorting out your differences.

Nick: *So you think you have a busy day, do you?*
Sally: *Well, at least I get everything done by the evening – not like you, bringing stuff home to work on every night.*
Nick: (contempt) *Oh yeah, you're so clever aren't you. It must be really hard to get a few nappies changed and do a bit of dusting in time for the seven o'clock news.*
Sally: *Stop patronising me, will you.*

The way Nick talks indicates a long standing difference between this couple. This is a well-worn track that they have been down before, always with the same result. And the more it goes on, the less Nick understands and the more fed up he becomes, while Sally grows equally infuriated by his refusal to take her concerns seriously, and the lack of respect he shows for her. If this kind of contemptuous talk happens every day, they will move further apart and risk losing any positive feelings they once had for each other.

Refusing to enter into a discussion

This is a defence mechanism, used more often by men than women, that leads to total breakdown in communication. If one partner totally refuses to engage with the other, either by taking the 'problem, what problem?' approach, or by physically removing themselves from the conversation, there is no chance of the couple resolving their differences.

Sally: *You knew we'd have to leave the party at 11 to get back for the babysitter. So why did you make such a song and dance about it – you made me feel really embarrassed.*

Nick: (refusing to enter discussion) *Huh* (picks up news-
    paper and retreats behind it).
Sally: *Up until then we'd had a good evening, and then you
    went and spoilt it. I wish you'd stick to what we agree.*
Nick: (Remains behind newspaper, says nothing).
Sally: *Nick, come on, talk to me.*
Nick: (Still doesn't respond).
Sally: *Oh, I give up.*

BETTER WAYS TO ARGUE

Slipping into an argument can be as comfortable as slipping
into a well-worn pair of shoes – it all feels so familiar. Just
because your patterns of arguing tend to repeat themselves,
however, doesn't mean you have to stick with them for life.
There are better ways to handle disagreements, so you
stand a chance of arriving at a solution that suits you both.

Start amicably

Next time there's a burning issue that you want to have out
with your partner, think about what you want to say
beforehand, then start the conversation amicably. Launch in
angrily and you're doomed to failure.

Jaspal and Suuki often argued about money.

*Whenever the credit card bill arrived I'd rip it open and just
start yelling at him for overspending. The same thing happened month in, month out. Then one month, when I
realised the bill was due any day, I said, 'Let's talk about the
bill before it arrives and try not to have a row about it. What
we need to do is work out a spending limit that's OK for both
of us.' It really took the wind out of his sails, but we did sit
down together and do some sums, so that when the bill
arrived we could say, Next month, it'll be better.*

Seek to understand your partner's reactions

This is where hidden agendas come in, if your partner is reacting to something other than what you are supposedly fighting about.

Darlene and Chris both had children from previous marriages. Darlene's lived with them, while Chris's lived with their mother and he saw them on an irregular basis. Darlene says:

My children were always in the wrong with Chris. They couldn't do anything right; it was pick, pick, pick. For the first couple of years we were together there was terrific strain on us because of his attitude to my children. But gradually I started to understand that because he doesn't see his own children that often, he thinks they're perfect. And he misses them, and he was taking those feelings out on my children. Until then, we'd had loads of rows with me saying, 'You mustn't be like that with my kids.' I changed tack, and started saying, 'I think you were being unfair when you said Elspeth doesn't do anything in the house, because she does' – and pointing out what she did do. That way, I could let him know how I felt, without attacking him. In time things have improved, and he is more tolerant of my two now.

Be responsible for your own emotions

Back to hidden agendas again. When there's a disagreement, ask yourself, why are you responding as you are? Have some other feelings been aroused by the current row? Heather and Joseph used to have blazing rows whenever he fancied a lunchtime drink at the weekend.

I remember shrieking, 'I won't have you drunk in front of the baby,' and he looked at me flabbergasted and said, 'I was only going to have a pint . . .' My problem stemmed right

*back to my own childhood, when my father used to have
heavy drinking bouts, which scared the life out of me and my
brother. I always found it hard to believe that Joseph would
stop at just one pint, because my father never could.*

Learn to compromise

In the best solutions to rows, both sides come away feeling
that they have got something they wanted. This rarely happens unless both are willing to give a bit, and not stick too
rigidly to the outcome they wanted. Discuss what you both
want, listen properly, then try to thrash out a solution that
leaves you both feeling satisfied.

Jenny and Adrian used to row because he wanted to play
rugby every Saturday afternoon.

*I wanted him to spend those afternoons helping me do the
weekly shop with the baby, but he was adamant that he didn't
want to give up his one regular sports session. In the end we
agreed that we would do the weekly shop together on
Saturday mornings, which meant getting ourselves organised a bit earlier in the day than we would do usually – a very
simple solution that worked well for both of us, and didn't
demand too much of a sacrifice from anyone.*

HOW ROWS AFFECT CHILDREN

Before children, you can row all night, chuck plates, shout
and swear and no one else need know about it except the
two of you. Things change, once there's a baby wailing in
its high chair as you swap insults. Children are very quick
to pick up on disharmony between their parents and may
voice their objections loudly.

Yet real life means that inevitably there will be times

when children do witness rows. Counsellor Denise Knowles, says that parents need to learn how to argue and how to resolve arguments.

It's OK to disagree as long as you resolve it via negotiation and compromise. You're giving children the message that the world doesn't end because you disagree, you can make it up again, and there are good ways to do that. In effect, you're teaching them how to argue constructively, and that's a very valuable lesson for life. Don't be afraid to let children see you apologise, either. Knowing how to admit you were wrong, and say sorry sincerely, takes maturity, and is another valuable skill to demonstrate in front of your children. Remember, though, that when the argument is about how to handle the children themselves you should always present a united front. Sort out your disagreements on this one when the children are not around.

HANDLING SERIOUS PROBLEMS

It is a sad fact that, according to the most recent figures, over 150,000 British children are affected by divorce every year. Of these, one-quarter are aged less than five when their parents split up, and most are under ten. Few people would advise someone in a deeply unhappy relationship to stick with it just for the sake of the children but, at the same time, parents need to beware of giving up too soon, without making their best efforts to save the relationship. Many, if not all, couples go through serious crises in their relationships, and having children can be the straw that breaks the camel's back. Yet it can be possible to get back on course and emerge stronger and happier than you were before.

Suppose your arguments signal a deeper unhappiness with the way your life as a couple is going? If your conflicts stem from deep-rooted, long-term problems, which existed long before you had children, it may be much harder to break the pattern.

_____ **Think about it** _____

- Do you feel that your lives are moving in totally different directions – perhaps one wants the stability of family life, while the other hankers after freedom and independence?

- Do you argue constantly, without ever making any headway in solving your problems?

- Do alcoholism, drug abuse, physical violence or other destructive behaviours form a part of your relationship?

- Is one of you being unfaithful?

- Does either of you frequently think or talk about leaving the other?

If any of these are true for you and your relationship, you need to find support and help. This could come from friends or family, or you might decide to see a relationship counsellor. Relate can offer long-term counselling if that's what you want, but there is also a counselling helpline and the possibility of one-off troubleshooting sessions. A quick shot of support and help, when it is most needed, can see you through a crisis and set you back on track again.

Family mediation

If ultimately you do decide to separate, you can get help from family mediation services. Mediation takes place privately and informally with a trained mediator who helps both of you understand each other's concerns and find a solution that is agreeable to everyone in the family. See page 217 for more information about these services.

_____ **In brief** _____

- It ain't what you say, it's the way you say it, that indicates how destructive your rows are likely to be.

- Don't despair if fights repeat endlessly – patterns can be broken.

- It's no bad thing for children to witness arguments, as long as they see that you always make it up later.

- Some problems have no easy solution.

Chapter 17

FINDING A WAY OUT OF DEPRESSION

For the last two months I have been in the grip of depression, which culminated this afternoon with a couple of hours of blackest misery. Life seems so chaotic – the house is a mess, coping with the children makes practical matters difficult; just getting the washing done or cooking a meal is such an effort. I can't see any possibility of ever getting back to work – how would I do it? And I don't feel well. I wonder if there's something really wrong with me. Miss my friends, wish we hadn't moved – it's all too much to bear. Jo

Maybe it's not so surprising that numerous women, and a fair number of men, feel depressed after having a baby. Life changes so profoundly after a baby is born and many women are also completely exhausted for the first few months. Doctors have tended to blame depression on hormonal influences, and certainly hormone levels can and do fluctuate and alter after birth. Increasingly, though, it is being realised that there are many other factors which can contribute to the onset of depression.

Around 80 per cent of women experience a few days of the 'baby blues', while some develop postnatal depression. The Association for Postnatal Illness (see page 216) believes that one in five new mothers is affected, but it's likely that the actual number is higher, since postnatal depression isn't always recognised until it has passed, so sufferers don't always ask for treatment. At the top end of the scale of depression is postnatal psychosis, which, although rare, is a serious condition requiring hospital treatment.

BABY BLUES

The baby blues are a spell of high emotion often mingled with mild depression, which hits most new mothers, usually starting when the baby is a few days old and clearing in days or, at most, weeks. A woman with the baby blues might feel:

- very emotional; euphoric one minute, in tears the next
- depressed for no obvious reason and unable to 'cheer up'
- anxious, tense, worried over small problems
- generally unwell, or suffering from physical pains with no apparent cause
- extremely tired, no energy, but unable to sleep even when baby is sleeping

In the midst of everything else that is going on, it's easy to forget that your hormones are on a switchback, which can profoundly affect the way you feel. Don't think you're going crazy when you start bursting into tears, or feel totally exhausted but can't sleep. It helps enormously if you and your partner recognise what is going on, and remember that it is a passing phase.

_____ **Try this** _____

Men can do a lot to help their partner if she has the blues.

- When things seem bad, gently remind her that she will soon feel better.

- Listen to her, reassure her that her feelings will soon pass. Be patient and tactful, and don't dismiss her feelings as unimportant or silly.

- See that she gets as much rest as possible. Take over with the baby for an hour or two while she has a lie down. Rest is beneficial even if she doesn't sleep.

MEN CAN GET DEPRESSED TOO

Up to 10 per cent of new fathers feel depressed after their babies are born, and if your partner is depressed there's an even higher chance that you will feel down as well. There are numerous reasons for this. Men often feel under a lot of pressure when they become fathers: they have new responsibilities; their partner may be less able to provide emotional support, or may be turning to them for support; there may be money worries or other problems; and trying to cope with work in the midst of all this can be the last straw.

Depression can make you feel generally low and unable to concentrate or enjoy life. You can lose your appetite, suffer from insomnia and be burdened by worries. It's tempting to ignore these feelings, especially in a culture where men are still traditionally expected to be strong. Don't resort to escaping into work or drinking too much. You've a much better chance of getting over your depression if you get some help.

―――――――――――― **Try this** ――――――――――――

- Talk to your partner about how you feel.

- Confide in a friend who has children, or ring a helpline such as Parent Line (see page 218) for support and advice.

- Your GP may be able to suggest other ways of getting help.

POSTNATAL DEPRESSION

Postnatal depression in women can emerge in two ways. It may start life as a phase of baby blues which, instead of lifting after a few days, gradually deepens and gets worse.

With other women, PND develops slowly over weeks or months, commonly appearing when the baby is between four and six months old.

Katya suffered from postnatal depression from her baby's birth until he was five months old, but didn't immediately realise what was going on.

To start with I put my feelings down to tiredness. Finlay was a fretful baby right from birth, and I often felt that I wasn't coping very well. As time went by, I realised I was feeling worse rather than better. Although Finlay was becoming more settled, I still had this terrible churning feeling inside all the time, and had spells where everything seemed totally bleak. The crunch came when he was about four months old. My husband came home one evening. Finlay was crying, and I shoved him into my husband's arms and ran down to the end of the garden. I remember screaming and crying 'Take him away, take him away.' When I'd calmed down I knew that this was a crisis – I had to get help, and I saw my GP the next day.

Louella came to Relate when her baby Karl was eight months old. She had recovered from a bout of postnatal depression, but found that her relationship with her husband Marc had changed and they were now very distant with each other. Her counsellor says:

She felt that her depression had been sparked off by the fear she had felt that she would never be alone again. She found the constant demand of the baby, and his need for her to be there all the time, very stifling, almost claustrophobic. Things were made much worse because the family had just moved for Marc's job, and so Louella had no friends or relatives nearby to turn to. Marc hadn't understood what was going on when she became depressed and had withdrawn his support.

It can be hard for partners to grasp just what it feels like to be depressed. The counsellor continues:

We sometimes ask too much of our partners. They are not our counsellors and can't always offer the support we need. In this case, the postnatal depression had had a very destructive effect on the relationship. There needs to be more awareness of just how far-reaching postnatal depression can be, and more help available for couples who are struggling with it.

Why does postnatal depression happen?

Hormone levels possibly have something to do with it, but there may be one or more circumstances in your life which make postnatal depression more likely.

_____ **Think about it** _____

PND is more likely to affect women who:

- have been having relationship problems before the baby was born
- had a very stimulating job and find it hard to adjust to motherhood
- experienced a difficult birth
- have previously suffered from depression
- are extremely tired because their baby sleeps badly
- have other difficulties or problems and not enough support

Recognising postnatal depression

PND can manifest itself in various ways. Although there is a long list of possible symptoms, each woman is different and while some will experience all the symptoms, others will show only one or two.

Frequently the woman herself doesn't recognise or accept that anything is wrong. She may explain her symptoms away, sometimes putting them down to her own inadequacy as a mother, or just dismissing them as being unimportant or normal. Partners and family should be on the lookout for symptoms if they suspect that a woman is depressed. Often, recognising that there is a problem and acknowledging it openly is the first step towards getting better.

Symptoms of postnatal depression include the following.

- Feeling depressed or rejected, very miserable for no obvious reason and tearful.
- Lethargic, unable to cope with looking after baby or household chores.
- Loss of interest in personal appearance.
- Anxiety and panic. May be worried about own health and fear serious illness, worry about baby's wellbeing, or be fearful for other family members.
- Obsessional thoughts. Kate Figes describes these feelings in her book *Life After Birth*:

  When each of my babies was just weeks old, I saw dangers everywhere: a kitchen knife could so easily be plunged into her stomach, too great a squeeze could break her neck, or a pillow could so easily smother her. I knew that I would never kill my babies, but the images were so vivid and frequent that they were frightening and felt uncomfortably close to madness at times, for I had no control over them and couldn't prevent them from coming.

- Loss of concentration. Memory may be very poor, may feel hopelessly disorganised. Chris recalls:

  I couldn't read a book, couldn't even glance at the paper. I couldn't get past the first sentence without losing the thread. On one of the worst days, I sat on my own all afternoon with the baby on my lap, just looking at her, with huge tears rolling slowly down my face, thinking about how awful I felt and how there was no way out. I thought about killing myself and the baby – it's horrifying, looking back at it, but at the time it seemed perfectly logical – life was too awful to go on, she needed me, so if I went she'd have to come too. While this was going on I also knew that I wasn't actually going to harm myself, or her, but I certainly considered it as a way out of the dreadful pain I was in.

- Loss of appetite and insomnia. Unable to sleep, even if prescribed sleeping tablets. Depression may be worse at night.
- Loss of libido. This in itself puts a strain on a couple's relationship, especially if the cause is not recognised. Chris says:

One of the biggest problems for us was sex, or rather the total lack of it. By the time the baby was four months old we'd only attempted it twice and it had been hopeless. I was still a bit sore from the episiotomy and was also exhausted – Martha was a very bad sleeper and I hadn't had more than three uninterrupted hours sleep since she was born. But I think it was the depression that caused a complete loss of libido, just nothing there at all. And because of that there was an estrangement between me and my husband that lasted for months and months.

Treating postnatal depression

The good news is that postnatal depression is an illness like any other and, like any other illness, can be treated and cured. The vast majority of women with PND make a full recovery.

The first step is to recognise that something is wrong.

Men who think their partner may have PND can try to persuade her to seek help. If she refuses, then go and see your GP on her behalf. The doctor can then arrange to make a home visit to assess the situation. Don't struggle on hoping that the depression will cure itself.

There are various types of 'talking treatments' that for many women are as effective as taking antidepressants. According to the Health Visitors' Association, sessions with a trained health visitor or counsellor can be extremely helpful, and are often all that is needed.

Cognitive therapy is another possible treatment, which helps you understand and change negative thought patterns. Your GP can refer you to a cognitive therapist. Psychiatric help is also often used to help treat PND and again, your GP can refer you to a suitably qualified psychiatrist. Lindsay remembers:

The big change for me came when I told Matt that I thought I was suffering from depression and needed help. He'd been worried, but hadn't known what to do. We saw our GP together, and just acknowledging that there was a problem and having it taken seriously helped me enormously. My GP referred me to a psychiatrist who visited me twice at home. I poured everything out to her and it was as if a weight lifted off me as I talked. In between her first and second visit I knew that the depression was receding, and after a couple more weeks the bad days had stopped altogether.

Antidepressant drugs are the other avenue of treatment for PND and can be used on their own or alongside one of the 'talking' treatments. Drugs such as Prozac are non-addictive and can be highly effective in lifting depression. Mandy had PND after Kimberley was born.

I couldn't be bothered to get out of bed, wash my hair or eat. Eventually my husband told the health visitor what was happening and she arranged for my doctor to visit me at home. She prescribed Prozac and after about ten days things started to seem easier. In a month or so I felt back to my normal self and came off the drugs. They were a life-saver for me.

_____ **Try this** _____

If you want to help someone with postnatal depression:

- be understanding. It takes time to cure PND, and a depressed woman needs understanding and support until she recovers

- take on some of the running of the household. Let her do as much or as little as she wants

- look after her, by making sure she gets plenty of rest and encouraging her to eat and drink properly

- make sure she does not spend too much time on her own

- reassure her frequently that she will recover

- don't tell her to pull herself together, or try to talk her into feeling differently. Her feelings are not under her control at the moment

If you have postnatal depression:

- acknowledge your feelings and talk about them

- be kind to yourself and take it easy. Accept offers of help

- try to get out of the house every day. Gentle exercise and fresh air can help to lift your mood

- leave your baby with your partner or a trusted friend and take an hour or two for yourself to do something you really enjoy

WHEN DEPRESSION IS MORE SERIOUS

There is a rare form of PND, called postnatal psychosis, which affects about one woman in every 500, and usually sets in during the first three months after the birth.

Symptoms of postnatal psychosis can include:

- intense exhaustion, sleeping for hours at a time or even all day
- long bouts of crying
- extreme anxiety and tension
- strange behaviour, manic cheerfulness
- paranoia
- hallucinations
- suicidal thoughts
- thoughts of harming the baby

A woman with this condition needs urgent help. Patients with postnatal psychosis are hospitalised, with their babies, during treatment, which may take weeks or even months to be effective.

LIFE AFTER DEPRESSION

Many women who've been through an episode of depression are fearful of experiencing another if they go on to have more children. There is no accurate research available on the real likelihood of recurrence. All that can be said is that some women do have postnatal depression a second or third time, while others don't.

If you have had one episode of postnatal depression, you are at least well-equipped to prepare yourself for the possibility of the same thing happening again. The Association for Postnatal Illness (see page 216) advises women to make plans in case they do become depressed again and to arrange for plenty of support to be available when they are most likely to need it. Being alert for symptoms and getting treatment swiftly will help to make any depression that does occur shorter-lived.

Depression after childbirth is very common and doesn't reflect badly on the sufferer in any way. It is possible to get very effective treatment, so if you are feeling low don't go on fighting your way through each day. The sooner you ask for help, the sooner you can start to recover.

In brief

- Baby blues are soon over. Postnatal depression goes on and on.

- Notice your feelings and take them seriously.

- There are very effective treatments, so don't delay getting help.

- Men can also become depressed after a baby is born.

PART FIVE
AS CHILDREN GROW

Chapter 18

BABIES BECOME TODDLERS

Nine o'clock on a cold January night. I've just come down-stairs from settling Sarah – she woke up and couldn't find her teddy. The baby's asleep for a change – I can hear him breathing gently over the alarm – wonderful sound. Phew! This is my first chance to sit down in peace and quiet all day. What I'd really like to do is put my feet up with a glass of wine and the paper, but I suppose I'll have to have a bit of a clear up, because the room . . . Well, you can certainly tell who lives here. This is what's on the floor: a fur purse shaped like a bear's face, one navy baby sock, A–Z atlas, three videos out of their boxes, two remote controls, bottle with half an inch of milk, empty cup, empty yoghurt pot, apple core, small plastic panda wearing a green boiler suit, damp J-cloth, comic, two letters (unanswered), some crayons, a gold foil party trumpet, four used tissues, a multi-coloured stuffed octopus, four soft blocks, Playmobil slide with plastic person, address book, jumper with baby-sick garnish . . . And in the midst of it all I sit, scribbling, not unhappy, but paralysed with exhaustion, wondering what happened to that nice tidy house I once lived in. Trish

Babies, at least when they're tiny, stay where you put them. It's not too hard to keep your home looking as if adults live in it. But once children become mobile and start to have more and more ideas about what they want to do and how they want to do it, they take over every room of the house.

Regiments of plastic toys march round the edge of the bath, toys and puzzles seed themselves across living rooms, kitchen floors disappear under a layer of dropped and rejected food. There are booster seats, steps beside the loo and by the bath, car seats, buggies. There are things *everywhere*.

Toddlers are delightful. They can be incredibly funny, extremely loving, immensely rewarding. They sop up learning like a sponge and you can see them develop from day-to-day. You can reap the rewards of time spent teaching them about the world. But they are also very hard work.

Not only do toddlers fill homes with equipment and belongings, but they are vociferous as well. Adults can chat happily and uninhibitedly in front of a contented baby. Toddlers demand to join in, ask what things mean, take on board whispered arguments or rude words and repeat them at inappropriate moments. They like to watch the same video, over and over again, and they like you to watch it with them. They also like to repeat games and songs. You can't strap a toddler into the back of the car and forget about her, as you can a baby. Toddlers want to listen to tapes in the car, loudly and repeatedly. Toddlers are messy. They like to get their fingers into things like porridge, yoghurt or paint and spread them around, over themselves, over the floor, over the cat. They never put things away.

Toddlers like your belongings just as much as their own. One mother said, despairingly:

I work at home, but Bethany's into everything. Now that she can open the door of my office, I can't leave papers on my desk any more because she shuffles them, or scribbles on them. Everything has to go up on high shelves. It drives me nuts.

Toddlers can provoke such a range of feelings in their parents. They inspire deep love and protectiveness, they are totally amazing in the way they develop from a tiny blob of a baby into a walking, talking, thinking, reasoning person with a distinct personality. But they can also drive you to frustration, boredom, rage. And they are highly efficient at absorbing all your time and energy, so there's little left to give to your own relationship.

SAY NO, AND MEAN IT

We've seen a complete turn around from previous centuries, when children were seen and not heard. Their needs, if considered at all, came a poor second to the pressing demand on adults to provide for them, or, if wealthy, to continue their social life uninterrupted. Even a generation ago, mothers got on with the cooking or housework and children amused themselves, or were shooed out of the house to play in the street or park.

Not any more. Child psychologist Asha Phillips, author of *Saying No: Why It's Important For You and Your Child*, believes that in our society children always come first.

Too often, that translates into a way of living where parental needs are completely consumed by children. Uninterrupted sleep and adult leisure become luxuries. But it isn't healthy to turn children into little emperors.

Naturally, there are times when a child's needs must come first. Often though, by saying yes when you know you would be better off saying no, you are creating a child who knows that the world revolves around him, and that no one else's needs matter.

For example, suppose you are trying to have a conversation with your partner and your two-year-old gets restless and starts whingeing. You give him sweets to keep him happy. He eats them, then demands more. You say no, but he cries, so you give in. Those sweets disappear too, and once again he tries to interrupt you. In desperation you offer more sweets, he flings them on the floor and starts to cry, you shout at him . . .

Most parents of toddlers will recognise the pattern. Keep repeating it, and your time together will be constantly eroded. Children *can* learn to wait their turn and respect other people's rights. It won't happen overnight, but gradually it can happen.

Try this

- First and foremost, remember that you have as much right to an adult conversation as the child has to your attention. In order that everyone is reasonably satisfied, there will have to be a compromise. Say, 'I need to talk to Daddy for five more minutes, and then I'll play with you. Can you go and choose a puzzle we can do together?' This approach works well, especially when children are a little older, as long as they learn to trust you to stick to your side of the bargain.

- You are in control, not the child. Be firm and when you say no, mean it.

- Start this approach when children are very young and be consistent.

- Support each other in the way you handle your child. This is vital. It is pointless one saying no, if the other then weakens. Small children are clever and quickly suss out which parent is the soft touch. Agree on the boundaries and stick to them.

- Distraction often works wonders with small children. Spending a couple of minutes setting up something for them to do, like colouring a picture for you, can win you several uninterrupted moments to yourselves.

BE ADAPTABLE

You can save yourselves a lot of grief by adapting your lives to suit the needs of your child. If you try and stick rigidly to routines that worked fine when you were just a couple, or when your toddler was a baby, you are in for a disappointment.

Mealtimes

When to eat? Organising meals to suit everyone takes a lot of flexibility, and the solutions alter as children get older. In *Balancing Acts*, Victoria, mother of George and Harry, tells how she created a family mealtime.

One of the ways to cut down on menial tasks was to cook just one evening meal at six-thirty, instead of cooking one meal for the children and another later on for us. Feeding the children, putting them to bed (a major war in itself), clearing up their supper things, cooking a new meal for us, then clearing up again, took four hours of the evening and I was lucky if I made it in time to sit down for the ten o'clock news. Now, we get the worst of it over in the early evening so there is some time later on to talk or read. If my husband doesn't get home in time for the evening meal, he cooks for himself.

Vicky's solution is very practical. The downside is that the evening meal isn't a very restful occasion, with two small tired children to contend with, but the reward is more free time later in the evening.

Amanda tried a different tack.

For me, an evening meal with my husband is a kind of watershed, marking the beginning of the adult part of the day. Also, the children don't like the kind of food we have – they can't cope with whole fish, for example, don't like spicy

*things, and prefer bland food. They're perfectly happy to
have the same dozen or so dishes over and over again.*

*I manage it by feeding the children early, around five-thirty.
While they're eating, I make preparations for our meal, peeling
or chopping vegetables, making sauce, getting everything as
nearly ready as possible. Then I play with the children for a while
before bathing them and putting them to bed. On a good night
my husband gets home around seven, so he can get stuck in with
bathing and reading while I nip down and put the pasta on or
whatever. Between us we can get a meal on the table before
eight. Oh, and the deal is that I cook and he does the washing up.*

*I am finding that as my eight-year-old daughter gets older,
she stays up later, but I have made a pact with her that
Daddy and I have half an hour to eat together which is our
time to catch up on the day, and she plays in her room or
reads while we do this, and then I read to her before she puts
her light out at eight-thirty. So far it has worked well, and for
me it's worth having a labour-intensive couple of hours in the
early evening to get my grown-up meal later on.*

The key to Amanda's success is that she and her husband
work together to get what they want. It takes a lot of co-
operation and goodwill to get these kind of arrangements
working, but everyone stands to gain from them.

LIFE IN TODDLER LAND

If one partner, still most often the man, is away from home
at work all day, it can be hard for him to understand just
why the house looks like a battlefield when he gets home,
and why he has to leap straight in and help with the
children the minute he steps through the door. If you've
never had to look after a small child single-handed, it can be
hard to imagine what it's like.

It's a good idea for mothers to take a day off sometimes, so that fathers can find out just what does go on during a normal toddler day. In *Balancing Acts*, Victoria says

Once I left my 18-month-old and my husband to their own devices while I travelled to London for a meeting. At that stage, the baby was into everything. I couldn't turn my back for a minute. I think my husband thought it would be a doddle – I knew he thought I made too much fuss about what a handful George was, but when I rang him to make sure everything was OK, he yelled down the phone, 'You've got to come back at once – I just found him climbing up the bookcase and I haven't been able to finish a phone call since you left.'

It's good for everyone to have time not just to themselves, but time as a couple, as well as time spent looking after children alone. Yes, it does take organisation, but it's organisation well worth doing.

Fathers doing the caring

A growing number of fathers do take on the full-time care of their small children. Franco looked after his daughter Olivia while his wife returned to her well-paid job. Although he enjoyed the experience, it wasn't as easy as either he or his wife had imagined.

This has been the most challenging and satisfying time of my life. Yet my relationship with Maxine has been severely strained. Our expectations of each other did not coincide and my idea of a clean house did not match hers. She found it very hard to go to work knowing she would miss another day of Olivia's development. The resentment led to rows. We didn't have the time or energy to talk about how our lives had changed.

Whoever cares for the children, boredom, isolation and frustration can all take their toll. These emotions are part of the package of parenting, but unless partners support each other and recognise the strains and stresses, they can prove very damaging to a relationship.

ANOTHER ROLE CHANGE

Cheryl, whose daughter was born when she was 43, found it more difficult than expected to escape from traditional roles and expectations.

We both grew up in the Fifties, in traditional families with a working father and a mother who stayed at home. We still carry some of those assumptions despite all the social change since. Our family backgrounds have also affected our attitudes on how our daughter should be cared for. My husband had a twin brother and another slightly older brother, so he always had someone to play with. As a result, he seems to assume that the role of parent is just a matter of being around, whereas I tend to see it more in terms of interacting/playing with/chatting to our daughter.

Our own experience of being a child is a powerful influence on our ideas of what parenting is all about, as Cheryl discovered. Like it or not, we do tend to repeat at least something of what we know from the past, and it can take a lot of insight and determination to change that.

'I want Mummy'

What's more, children have their own ideas about who should do what when it comes to looking after them.

Sam is very 'Mummy-ish' at the moment — Daddy isn't allowed to bath her. If she wakes in the night she wants

Mummy, and if Daddy goes she cries even louder until I rouse myself and go to her. Angie

Nor are these preferences peculiar to very young children. Older ones work out which parent is the best bet, depending on their needs at that moment. Six-year-old Martha says:

Daddy's humungously good fun. He'll play football or piggy-in-the-middle with us when he comes home. And if you ask him to play he always says yes. Mummy won't always stop and play if she's busy. But she's lovely and cuddly. I like her to tuck me up and read to me at night, and play quiet games with me. If I'm sad, or I hurt myself, or I'm not very well, then I really, really want Mummy.

Think about it

If one parent is jealous of the other's bond with a child, or feels ousted if the child sometimes prefers the other parent, problems can arise.

- Children are very good at playing one parent off against the other, once they realise, even subconsciously, that something about their relationship with their parents is creating a tension. Parents must stand firm and present a united front.

- Talk to each other about it, and try to understand what is happening from the child's point of view.

- Never be tempted to use your child's preference as a weapon in an argument with your partner.

- Sometimes a child needs more from one parent than from another, but these needs change as a child grows. If your child prefers your partner at the moment, enjoy the chance to have a break. Things even out in the end.

Fathers can get left out

Many mothers do take on the major childcaring role, and with a tiny breastfed baby this may be the only realistic option. As children get older, however, it's important that their dad also gets a chance to look after them and form a strong relationship, if he hasn't already done so. Sometimes, though, it can be extremely hard for a mother, who is used to having sole charge of the child, to let the father have a share in the caring.

Lynne and Eddy came to Relate when their little girl Saffron was two. The counsellor remembers:

Lynne knew that she'd always been a very anxious mother, and when Saffron was tiny she hadn't let Eddy do any of the looking after because she felt he wouldn't do it properly. The problem was that, as Saffron got older, this pattern hadn't changed. Eddy really wanted to get to know his daughter better, but whenever he tried to play with her or help her at mealtimes, Lynne was always hovering in the background, criticising, or snatching the spoon away saying, 'Let me do that.' He was left feeling totally useless and unwanted.

The counsellor helped Lynne and Eddy to tackle the problem in two ways.

First, Lynne had to realise that she could let go a bit, and that Eddy was perfectly competent to look after Saffron. Lynne was actually missing some of the things she used to do, like swimming, and letting Eddy help would free her to resume her weekly swim. She wasn't very happy with the existing situation, and felt it was unfair that she did everything for Saffron. In counselling, she gradually began to understand how she herself had created that situation, by not letting Eddy help. Once having realised what she was doing, she could try to change things. Eddy's job was not to give up, but to be a bit more assertive at staking his claim on Saffron, at the same time reassuring Lynne that he could manage. Little by little he began taking Saffron out, to the park or to see his mother. As Lynne saw that nothing disastrous was going to happen, she was able to loosen up and stop the constant criticism which was wrecking their relationship.

There was a third task for them, said the counsellor.

Their relationship was completely focused on the child – they had more or less stopped seeing themselves as a couple. Part of the reason was that Saffron stayed up all evening, so they rarely had time together. They agreed to try and establish an earlier bedtime for her, and to spend some of the time they gained talking to each other and re-establishing the good relationship they'd had before she was born.

EXTRA PROBLEMS

Life with a toddler is quite a struggle, even when the child has no health or behavioural difficulties. For those who have to face these challenges as well, the strain can be colossal. Rahila's story is told in *Balancing Acts*. Her son was born with cerebral palsy.

Friends still ask how long I took to come to terms with it. But there is no such finiteness. Even today I am coming to terms with it. It is only as a young child's life unfolds that you begin to see the full extent of his or her limitations. Thank God, it doesn't hit you all at once. When you are told as the mother of a three-month-old baby that the baby's brain has been damaged at birth, that he will be developmentally delayed, you don't think it means that he will never walk. You think it means he will sit at 18 months instead of six months. But today, when he's three-and-a-half years old and still has the functions of a newborn baby, I am grateful if someone says that he might sit independently by the age of eight.

In the face of a child's severe disability, a couple's relationship may end up right at the bottom of the heap. A Relate counsellor who has helped several couples in this situation, explains:

The effects of the disability can cause a terrific strain, and all the couple's time is taken up caring for the child. It is virtually impossible for couples to invest in their own relationship in the face of that demand, but it's important that they try. They need to keep their relationship strong for the child, as well as themselves. Whatever the situation, it's vital to find some respite care, whether just for an hour or two or longer, where the parents can spend time together. Apart from that, I advise them to go easy on themselves, keep their expectations realistic and take it day-to-day.

OVER BEFORE YOU KNOW IT

There's something about being a parent which makes time accelerate. Perhaps it's because the days become so crammed, or because children seem to fast-forward in front of your eyes as they grow and develop. The baby stage is over in a few months; the crawling, tottering almost-toddler is soon just a memory. Even young childhood has its own distinct phases. There's a world of difference between a lisping two-year-old, and an articulate four-year-old who, though not yet at school, is now definitely less dependent and on the brink of a whole new experience.

Whatever stresses and strains each stage brings, remember, it's not forever. Enjoy as much of it as you can, try not to let the happy, good times get swamped by the exhausting or dull sides. Having toddlers is an intense, demanding time in your life as a couple, but even a few years down the line you'll be saying, 'Do you remember . . .', and looking at photos or videos of small children who have gone already and been replaced by children in the next stage of growing up. Making a conscious decision to try and enjoy this stage – every stage – of your children's lives can help you to focus on the positive, rather than becoming overwhelmed by the negative.

In brief

- A demanding stage, but lots of fun.
- Don't let your needs as a couple be completely sidelined.
- Get into the habit of each taking over the children sometimes, and giving the other a total break.

Chapter 19

HAVING ANOTHER CHILD

The decision to have another child came out of the blue for me and Tom – we went away together on holiday, just the two of us, leaving Lily with Granny, and strangely enough that first taste of freedom made me rush home to have another! Tom was surprised, but was quickly convinced that it was something I really wanted. He tried to remind me how ill I'd been with Lily but frankly I wasn't listening, although there were times during the pregnancy when I wished I had. The sickness was worse than ever and lasted the whole pregnancy. Tom and Granny had to look after everything – it was a huge strain on them. The pregnancy and birth were horrendous, but the outcome was very happy – Jago, now three. Everyone, me included, said enough was enough! Gaynor

Just as with the decision to have a first child, making up your minds to try for another is often a fluctuating process. Some people start off with fixed ideas about the family they would like to have, but these can be shaken in the face of the reality. One mother says:

I'd always said I wanted four children until I had one. Then it was three years before I felt up to having another and after that – no more.

For others, it works the other way.

I used to say I'd have one child and be back at work in six months, but I was amazed to find how much I enjoyed

being a mother. We decided to have another baby after eighteen months, and that turned out to be twins. So now I've got three, and I've given up work until they're all at school.

Plans don't always turn out quite as you'd expected, and until you have one child, it's hard to predict how you will feel about having another.

WHAT TO CONSIDER

Having a second – or third – child is a decision based very much on the emotions, but one which also has to take into account a lot of practical factors.

Think about it

- Children cost money. Although you probably won't have to buy baby equipment again, second children cost just as much as the first when it comes to paying for child-care, feeding and so on.

- You may have to move house in order to gain more space, or invest in a bigger car.

- How would another pregnancy fit in with your working plans? Would your employer allow a second spell of maternity leave?

- Just as important as your employer's attitude are your own feelings. Could you cope with going back once you have two children? According to Rebecca Abrams, in her book *Three Shoes, One Sock and No Hairbrush*, 40 per cent of mothers-of-one who have returned to work cut their hours or drop work altogether after their second child is born.

- Pregnancy is tiring, and when you already have a child to look after, it becomes doubly so. Once the baby arrives, you have to contend with the weariness of broken nights, and still find the energy to care for your other child.

These are practical factors, with practical answers. If you are both committed to the idea of having another child, you'll do your best to find solutions. But what about the emotional side of having another child?

Think about it

- When you introduce another child into the family, all the relationships change. This can produce strains but can also be a good thing, as it removes the intense emotional focus from a single child.

- How would another child impact on the amount of time you spend together as a couple? Is your relationship strong enough to cope with the demands of another child? Is this something that both of you want?

- Perhaps you are now with a different partner from the one with whom you had your first child. How will having another child affect the family relationships that you have established?

- A common fear is that you will be unable to love another child as much as you love the first. Sue described a dream she had when she was expecting her second daughter.

   Pete and Katy, who was three, and I were sitting together on the sofa looking at this new baby in the cot, and not knowing what to do with it. That dream reflected my very real fears – I couldn't imagine how another child would fit in with us, because we already loved each other so much. The minute she was born I realised how stupid that was. Love isn't finite, you can always find more of it for another child. We just seemed to grow as a family to accommodate the new baby – it wasn't a problem. And I love the two girls just as much as each other.

REACHING AN AGREEMENT

The idea of having another child can be quite scary. Couples often waver, one minute thinking, OK, let's go for it, the next moment saying, 'Hang on . . .' If this describes you, think about *why* you are worried – what exactly are you afraid of?

Daniel and Jen came to Relate when their second child was nine months old because their relationship was collapsing fast. The counsellor unravelled what had been happening:

They had had a first child with no problems, Jen went back to work and everything seemed fine. What went wrong was that when Jen said how much she wanted a second child, Dan was ambivalent. Although he loved their first child, his life had been affected far more than he'd anticipated. He felt he'd lost his personal space, and was afraid of being pushed beyond his limits by the extra demands of rearing another child. He'd never really come out and said this though, he'd just been non-commital when Jen talked about having another baby. Jen admitted that she'd known he had doubts, but she stopped taking the pill regardless and got pregnant. During the pregnancy their relationship went downhill. After the baby was born she had found it hard to bond with him, partly because she realised that this child was putting intolerable pressure on the marriage. Subconsciously she blamed the child, even though she recognised that she was actually responsible for what had happened. She was also angry with Dan because he didn't give her enough support.

Dan on his part was livid, because their lives had been turned upside down by this new child to whom he wasn't fully committed. During counselling a lot of painful feelings were expressed, and they seemed to be understanding each other better, but I don't know what the outcome was. Certainly, I have known of marriages breaking up in this type of situation, and I would urge couples to talk through the implications of having another child before embarking on pregnancy, and listen properly to what each of them is saying. If one partner wants a child and the other doesn't, it can be very hard to find a compromise, but ignoring the difference can be equally disastrous in the long term.

Doubts and misgivings

It's very normal to feel uncertain about committing your-selves to the idea of having another child. If things are going well with the first one, then why rock the boat? Moniza and Al had always imagined that they would have a family of two, but after Patrick was born, they were both so exhausted that they decided that one child was quite enough. However, by the time Patrick was a year old he had become much more settled and was reliably sleeping for 12 hours every night. At 15 months he was playing, walking, starting to talk – his parents adored him, and they were far less tired than they had been in the early days, when the thought of having another child had felt overwhelming. Moniza writes:

Last night, while we were watching Patrick playing with his trains, Al suddenly said, 'It would be nice for him to have a brother or sister.' I said, 'I thought you didn't want another baby?' Al just smiled and we started talking about the possibility of another. I felt very excited and couldn't sleep all night.

A day or two later, however, that excitement had worn off.

I do have reservations (of course). I dread the idea of another sickly pregnancy like last time and also, which is very important, I don't like the way it all intervenes between me and Al. At the moment we're back together, but it's been hard getting here.

This couple spent six months edging round the idea of having another child, talking through the pros and cons, trying to decide what was the best thing to do. At last:

Feels as though the decision is made: to stop contraception after my next period and await events . . . I feel excited, emotional and so does Al. Strangely, I'm not thinking much about how life will change, coping with pregnancy, two children, tiredness. People do cope. And the love and tenderness you have for your child . . .

The important thing is that it's a decision to be made by two people, and it can't be rushed. Most couples wonder if they're doing the right thing when they embark on another pregnancy. One father of three says:

The idea of 'people, not things' has been very important to us. Yes, we'd have been better off, lived in a bigger house, had better holidays, if we hadn't had the second child, and then the third, but what we've gained is immeasurable. I would say to anyone dithering about having another child, that as long as they feel confident in their relationship with their partner, go ahead. Enjoy your children, play with them, share their activities, teach them, love them – do it together.

After all, in about 20 years they will have left home and you'll have more personal space than you know what to do with.

THE RIGHT GAP

What is the right gap to have between children? Easy. There isn't a right gap. There isn't one option that's easier than the others, and what suits one family won't suit another.

Having your family over a fairly short space of time is hard work, and puts a lot of strain on you as parents. That said, the worst of it is soon over and, with luck, two children close in age should prove to be good playmates. Some families have a five-year, six-year or even longer gap between children. This way, you have more time to devote to each child when tiny, but the children may be at very different stages and not relate particularly well. And it can be hard to regain time to yourselves as a couple.

Longer – sometimes much longer – gaps are by no means unusual, particularly in stepfamilies. Journalist Maureen Freely says the whole idea of planning a gap is laughable if you split up with the father of the first child and have your next with a different man. Then everything becomes hyper-complicated.

If (like me) you have two sets of older children, each travelling at different times between two different houses, and a set of younger children always resident in the house in the middle, there are so many variables at work that you will be doing advanced maths just to set the table.

If you are adopting a second child, you are unlikely to have any choice about the gap between children. Caroline and Bill decided a year after they'd adopted their first child, who by then was four, that they would like to adopt a sibling for her.

We had to go through the entire assessment procedure all over again, which took time, and then we waited over two years before a child became available. We'd nearly given up, then out of the blue we were told that there was a baby boy that we could have. We brought him home, just one week later.

_____ **Think about it** _____

- Maternal age is a deciding factor. After all, if you have your first child at 38, you don't have the luxury of waiting until number one's at school before you have another.

- Money – enough of it – is vital, and it can be helpful to spread the load by having a longer gap between the children. On the other hand, you might then stand to lose income over a longer period if you're less free to do paid work for several years.

- Think about work. How long a break do you want, do you want to go back to the same job, how will you organise childcare for two?

- Recent research concluded that a gap of 18–23 months between pregnancies was of the most benefit to the health of the unborn child. But even paediatricians don't think that you should let this kind of research dictate the way you space your family. The trouble with this gap is that the second child arrives just as the first is in the throes of the terrible twos.

_____

Dr Harvey Marcovitch of the Royal College of Paediatrics and Child Health is quoted as saying:

What matters most with a second pregnancy is not the health of the unborn, but whether you can afford another. I'd say, if you can stand it, have the second when your child is 18 months or less, and too young to feel ousted, or wait until they are three, out of nappies and ready for playgroup.

STOPPING AT ONE

For some couples, having just one child is the right solution. Rick says:

I was an only child and so was my wife. I can see that it might be fun to have siblings when you're a child but, because I never had them, I never missed them. Rowena and I are willing to spend a lot of time with Chlöe, and neither of us feel that having another child would be right for us.

There are many advantages to having one child – it's less demanding in terms of time and money than a larger number. Some single children wish for siblings, others don't. In the end, you have to do what feels right for you as a family.

Plans can go awry

It's all very well making plans to have a child, but ultimately the whole thing is down to nature, fate, or whatever you want to call it. None of us actually has the power to decide exactly when, or whether, our children will arrive. Helena says:

I didn't have Rachel until I was 37, but I conceived her straight away, had a trouble-free pregnancy and birth, and she was an easy baby. We decided that we would have another one pretty soon and I was so complacent – I remember even saying that we should avoid conceiving in March so that the baby wouldn't have a Christmas birthday. As time went on and on and no pregnancy, I realised I'd missed the boat.

Rachel's six now – life has moved on. I am sad about it, but will always be hugely grateful that we managed to have Rachel before it was too late.

Infertility problems that were not present first time around can appear when you try for a second pregnancy. It's also common for women to miscarry between pregnancies.

In the business of having children, nothing can be taken for granted. It helps enormously to have a supportive partnership, and be there for each other in good times and bad, whether you are facing disappointment, or the arrival of a new family member.

In brief

- Consider the emotional implications of increasing the family, as well as the practical ones.

- Doubts and misgivings are par for the course.

- Make a joint decision. Going ahead when only one of you really wants to is inviting trouble.

- Every age gap has its pros and cons. Don't worry about it – children adapt to their siblings whatever the difference in years.

AFTERWORD

The greatest thing you can do for your children, is love your partner.

Stephen Covey, author of
The Seven Habits of Highly Effective Families

If you take away one thing from this book, let it be the idea that the wellbeing of your relationship is crucial. It's not selfish to put time and effort into it, even if that means – as sometimes it will – that your children's desires have to take second place. They will reap the rewards right through their childhood and beyond, if you, their parents, show them what a lively, loving relationship looks like. If they see you disagree and resolve your disagreements; if they hear you talking and laughing together; if they are aware that you are physically affectionate, you are setting up powerful examples for them to take into their own relationships in adulthood. What you are doing, when you invest time and love in your own relationship, is of untold importance both now and in the future.

So don't ignore problems that niggle away, eroding feelings and leaving an underlying discontent. Tackle them, and do it soon and together. Don't tell yourself that you don't have the time – find that time. Don't risk letting your relationship gradually decline, or even dissolve.

Enjoy the pleasures that a family bring. Enjoy the fun and laughter, the messy house, the comings and goings. Enjoy the tender moments and the tough ones. Through it all, keep sight of what made it happen in the first place –

the fact that you loved each other enough to want a family together. Hold on to that thought, and build on it. Invest time and love in your relationship, and together you can build the stable and rewarding family life that you and your children deserve.

FURTHER HELP

ORGANISATIONS

Association for Postnatal Illness
145 Dawes Road, Fulham, London SW6 7EB. Tel: 020 7386 0868. Website: www.apni.org.com
Ring for telephone advice and an information pack. Mothers with the illness can be matched with a volunteer who has had postnatal depression and recovered and who can give one-to-one telephone support.

Central Registry
The Court Service, Family Administration Department, Children Branch – Room 2.11, First Avenue House, 42–49 High Holborn, London WC1V 6NP Tel: 020 7947 6936
Contact them for a free pack with which unmarried fathers can apply for parental responsibility. A change due in the law in late 2001, giving unmarried fathers who register their children's birth jointly with the mother full parental rights, will make this unnecessary.

Down's Syndrome Association
155 Mitcham Road, London SW17 9PG. Tel: 020 8682 4001. Website: www.downs-syndrome.org.uk
Offer support, information and advice. Ring them for information on local branches, information booklets and newsletter.

Family Mediation
Website: www.open.gov.uk/lcd/family/fammed.htm
This website gives information about what mediation services offer. There is no overall body regulating mediation, but the website gives details of organisations such as the Family Mediators Association, (tel: 020 7881 9400) that offer mediation, and can provide a list of mediators in your area.

Fathers Direct
Herald House, Lamb's Passage, Bunhill Row, London EC1Y 8TQ. Tel: 020 7920 9491. Email: mail@fathersdirect.com
Website: www.fathersdirect.com
Information and on-line magazine aimed specifically at fathers, on all aspects of parenting.

Issue (The National Fertility Association)
114 Lichfield Street, Walsall, WS1 1SZ. Tel: 01922 722 888.
Email: webmaster@issue.co.uk Website: www.issue.co.uk
Members are offered confidential telephone counselling, a range of factsheets and bookets, support and advice.

Maternity Alliance
45 Beech Street, London EC2P 2LX. Information line: 020 7588 8582. Email: info@maternityalliance.org.uk Website: www.maternityalliance.org.uk
A charity working to improve rights and services for all pregnant women, new mothers and their families. Can provide expert information and specialist legal advice on maternity benefits and rights at work. Also produce a range of publications on these and other aspects of parenthood.

Meet-a-Mum Association
77 Westbury View, Peasedown St John, Banff BA2 8TZ. Tel: 01761 433 598 (general enquiries), helpline (7pm–10pm, Mon–Fri): 020 8768 0123 Website: www.mama.org.uk
A nationwide group for mothers who are isolated or have postnatal depression. Offer group or one-to-one support.

National Childbirth Trust

Alexandra House, Oldham Terrace, Acton, London W3 6NH. Enquiry line (9am–5pm Mon–Thurs, 9am–4pm Fri): 0870 4448 707.

Website: www.nctpregnancyandbabycare.com

Information and practical support on all aspects of pregnancy, childcare and early parenthood. Antenatal classes and postnatal support groups. Ring enquiry line for details of local services.

National Family & Parenting Institute

430 Highgate Studios, 53–79 Highgate Road, London NW5 1TL. Tel: 020 7424 3471. Website: www.e-parents.org

A campaigning charity, working towards a more family-friendly society. Unable to offer telephone advice, but their website has lots of useful information for parents.

Parentline Plus

520 Highgate Studios, 53–79 Highgate Road, Kentish Town, London NW5 1TL. Free helpline: 0808 800 2222. Website: www.parentlineplus.org.uk

A charity providing a free helpline, parenting courses, information leaflets and a useful website.

Parents at Work

45 Beech Street, London EC2Y 8AD. Tel: 0207 628 3565.

Helpline for parents needing advice on working rights and benefits: 0207 628 2128. Email: info@parentsatwork.org.uk. Website: www.parentsatwork.org.uk

Helps parents balance work and home by providing information and advice on working family-friendly hours, carer's leave and childcare.

PIPPIN (Parents In Partnership-Parent Infant Network)

Administration: Tel 020 8519 8821
e-mail: tracy@pippin.org.uk Website: www.pippin.org.uk

PIPPIN is a national charity which trains professionals such as midwives and health visitors to deliver a new approach to preparation for parenthood through NHS antenatal and postnatal classes and support. PIPPIN's approach, which is internationally acclaimed, is based on extensive research into support for British couples becoming parents and has been shown to have proven benefits for couple, family and parent-infant relationships. Ask your GP, midwife or health visitor if PIPPIN is offered in your area, or contact the organisation direct for details.

RELATE
Herbert Gray College, Little Church Street, Rugby CV21 3AP. Tel: 01788 573 241
Relate offers counselling to adults who are experiencing relationship difficulties. To obtain the number of your local Relate centre look under 'Counselling' or 'Relate' in the Yellow Pages.

SANDS (Stillbirth and Neonatal Death Society)
28 Portland Place, London W1B 4LY. Tel: 020 7436 7940. Helpline (10am–3.30pm, Mon–Thurs): 020 7436 5881. Email: support@uk-sands.org Website: www.uk-sands.org
Support, advice, local support groups, leaflets and books for parents whose babies have died before, during or shortly after birth.

BOOKS

All these books have different insights to offer into the experience of becoming a parent.

A Better Woman: a Memoir Susan Johnson (Aurum, 2000)
Families and How to Survive Them Robin Skynner and John Cleese (Vermilion, 1997)

Family Business Essays on ways of juggling work and
    family life, edited by Helen Wilkinson (Demos, 2000)

Fatherhood Reclaimed Adrienne Burgess (Vermilion, 1997)

From Here to Maternity: Becoming a Mother Anne Oakley
    (Penguin, 1986)

Hey Yeah Right Get A Life short stories by Helen Simpson
    (Vintage, 2001)

How Love Works Steve and Shaaron Biddulph (Thorsons,
    2000)

Life After Birth Kate Figes (Penguin, 2000)

*The Mask of Motherhood: How Becoming a Mother
    Changes Everything and Why We Pretend It Doesn't*
    Susan Maushart (Penguin, 2000)

A Minor Adjustment Andrew Merriman (Pan, 1999)

Saying No: Why It's Important for You and Your Child
    Asha Phillips (Faber and Faber, 1999)

The 7 Habits of Highly Effective Families Stephen R. Covey
    (FranklinCovey, 1997)

The Seven Principles for Making Marriage Work John
    Gottman and Nan Silver (Weidenfeld & Nicolson, 1999)

*Three Shoes, One Sock & No Hairbrush: all you need to know
    about having your second child* Rebecca Abrams (Cassell,
    2001)

I am grateful to Jean Shapiro for the wisdom and insights
contained in her book, *A Child, Your Choice*, (Pandora,
1987) now out of print, but still very relevant.

Two other books, now unavailable, also provided much
food for thought: Roberta Israeloff's *Coming to Terms*,
(Corgi, 1987) and *Balancing Acts: On Becoming a Mother*,
(Virago, 1989) edited by Katherine Gieve.

INDEX

You may also be interested in the following Relate titles
published by Vermilion:

Better Relationships by Sarah Litvinoff

Staying Together by Susan Quilliam

Sex in Loving Relationships by Sarah Litvinoff

Starting Again by Sarah Litvinoff

Second Families by Suzie Hayman

Loving in Later Life by Suzy Powling and Marj Thoburn

Stop Arguing, Start Talking by Susan Quilliam

After the Affair by Julia Cole

Loving Yourself, Loving Another by Julia Cole

To obtain a copy, simply telephone TBS Direct on 01206 255800